Tempus ORAL HISTORY Series

Minchinhampton
and Nailsworth
voices

Henry Beale, brother of Dorothea who was headmistress of Cheltenham Ladies College, seen in the 'Big Room' at Hyde Court, around the time of the First World War. His granddaughter, Gladys, is a contributor to this book.

Tempus ORAL HISTORY *Series*

Minchinhampton and Nailsworth
voices

Compiled by
Katie Jarvis

TEMPUS

First published 2001
Copyright © Katie Jarvis, 2001

Tempus Publishing Limited
The Mill, Brimscombe Port,
Stroud, Gloucestershire, GL5 2QG

ISBN 0 7524 2242 1

Typesetting and origination by
Tempus Publishing Limited
Printed in Great Britain by
Midway Colour Print, Wiltshire

To my grandmother, Katie Dyson, whose stories and songs filled my childhood

Cover picture: *A group of motorcyclists assemble for an outing at Ralph Dee's garage on the Bath Road near Egypt Mill in the 1920s.*

Contents

Introduction

I feel as if I've been living between two worlds while writing this book. In one world, I've been dancing to the busy rhythm of Gloucestershire's hectic, polluted twenty-first century life; in the other, I've been strolling among the calm, quiet old streets, peopled by children playing with whip tops and iron hoops. These little tots, in their quaint pinafores and lace-up boots, move out of the road at the last minute when some trader, passing with his pony and trap, calls out to them.

Then they run after him, shouting and calling, hoping perhaps that something will drop off his laden cart, which they can take home with pride to their mothers.
Sometimes even now, as I walk down Minchinhampton's Tetbury Street, or on the Common, or down Nailsworth's Brewery Lane, I can still catch a glimpse of that lost world. Perhaps it's in the mellow Cotswold stone, unaltered in hundreds of years; maybe it's in the rolling Common grass, which still yields the secrets of its bulwarks and strange, standing stones. And so I've tried to creep up and grasp those tantalising images, and lay them down for posterity among the pages of this book.

I've been to see people for whom those memories live on with glistening clarity in their minds. I've sat, rapt, with my notebook and pencil, sometimes forgetting to write as they tell me stories of golden childhoods, where they were free to wander all day in the woods, gathering orchids and bluebells, without fear or time constraints. But for every one of these halcyon days, I must not forget the harder times that accompanied them. For waiting back at home were the mothers of ten children, washing with water from an outside tap, or even the nearest stream.

Was it such a hard life? I suspect, like nowadays, there were good times and bad: such things never change. But as one person pointed out to me, there was a quiet routine to life in those days. Children were bathed once a week. Washday was always Monday – and nothing but washing would be done on that day. Nowadays, my washing machine goes on every day. And bathing the children might be an easier task, but it's certainly a more frequent one. If I add up the number of times I perform these daily jobs, I probably wouldn't be saving any more time than if I organised my week in the same way as my forebears did.

And hardest of all, was the frequency of that unwanted visitor, Death. Mothers died in childbirth, or worn out with work; fathers, for whom holidays and days off were a far greater luxury than today, might not make it out of their forties. Even in the early days of the last Century, it was far from unknown for families to lose one or more children.
The stories which I have collected are not history in the conventional sense. History is about important dates, and people who changed the world. And yet each of the tales told within these pages illustrates vividly the days in between those important, landmark dates. Stan Dyer's story about the death of his mother – in the chapter Difficult Days – is a poignant illustration of how little consideration was often given to the feelings of children.

And on a happier note, that lovable rascal of a foreman who teased the ladies from the safety of his road trench (Earning a Living) would probably be up before a tribunal if he tried that today. Yet his jokes were taken in the spirit in which they were meant – with smiles all round.

Four of the people whose tales have been told, have sadly died. I've been able to retell their stories because they made tapes, and wrote down their memories. What a wonderful legacy that was for them to leave.

So as today's children come in from school, with history books in hand, get them to put their school bags down for just half an hour. Instead, take them onto your knee and weave them stories of your own childhood. Tell them the names of their great grandparents. Sing them the songs you used to sing. Explain to them about entertainment, before the days of television, computers and Gameboys.

It's your own history, and theirs too – individual history that belongs to no-one else but you. And if you don't pass it on, it will be lost forever among the winding streets and carriage wheels of yesteryear.

Katie Jarvis

Acknowledgements

I would like to say thank you to the following people. They have been so generous with their memories, their precious photographs, and their time. I think they know that I feel hugely in their debt: Gladys Beale, Dorothy Blair, Daphne Bruton, Herby Creed, Lilian Day, Alan Denman, Mabel Dullea, Iris and Stan Dyer, Georgie Edmunds, Winifred Glassonbury, Valerie Halland, Wilfred Hartley, Vera Harvey, Sara Hill, Alan Hughes, Sheila Jarman, Jessie Kirby, Ann Makemson, Betty Mills, Muriel Newman, Sylvia Phelps, Norman Phillips, Jackie Porter, John Pring, Lady Mary Rawlinson, Kathleen Sawyer, Vera and John Skone, Dave Smith, Joanna Trollope, Claire Uzzell, May and Norman Vick, Peter Vick, John Vosper, Diana Wall, Ivor and Mercy White, Tony Wilson, Margery Woodward, Marshall Woodward, Ron Woodward, Anne Woollcombe-Boyce.
And finally, to Ian, without whom…

An early view of The Weighbridge Inn, possibly from the 1940s.

Prologue

Ghosts from the Past

My grandfather, William Porter from Shortwood, had a strange experience. He had his horses and the dray, and he was coming along the Avening Road by John's Hole – a spring past the Weighbridge. He reckoned his horses just stopped dead. He got out and saw that they were foaming at the mouth. He calmed them down, and had just got back into his cart when they suddenly bolted towards Nailsworth and didn't stop running until they got to Newmarket. A policeman saw him coming through the town, and he said to my grandfather, 'Never drive like that again!' My grandfather explained what had happened – though he always said that he never saw anything himself.

But it is said that, years ago, there was a coal mine on the bank where this happened. A man was supposed to have hung himself there, and people said you could hear the chains rattling sometimes. Maybe the horses were more sensitive to things like that.

Vera Skone (née Clarke), born 1927

CHAPTER 1
Golden Days of Childhood

John Hall, from Hall's Bakery in Minchinhampton, delivering bread to May Vick's Tetbury Street house. May's daughter, Pat, sits on the higher step.

A Ride on the Hay Cart

Everybody knows me as May, but my first name is Dorothy – I've never been called Dorothy, even as a child. I lived with my grandfather, William Beard, down Well Hill. In those days, there were no social services, so my mother, Lilian, had to go away to work. She went to Lower Slaughter to work as a domestic. I never went to see her – you towed the line with the gentry, and I wouldn't have been allowed over there. If my mother had a week off, or a weekend, she'd come home then, but I never really saw much of her.

When I was little, The Shard in Well

Hill was a farmhouse, and the people there had the name 'Royle'. They were good farmers, and we always went to play in their fields. There were only three of us. One of us was a boy who lived in one of the houses below. We only had hay making once a year then, and you could always guarantee good weather. The young won't believe me, but we used to have long, hot summers. They cut the hay and made it into big haycocks. As long as we behaved and didn't knock them over, we were allowed to play in them. I used to take a bottle of cold tea, and bread and jam, and spend all day there. We were all given a ride home on the hay cart, and it smelled lovely. In those days, you could say 'Next week we'll go on a picnic', because you knew it would be glorious weather.

A Captain Denne bought The Shard afterwards, with his sister. We didn't like him. They stopped us going down to play.

It was wonderful living down Well Hill. We had beautiful gardens – we could look over Gatcombe. Colonel Ricardo lived there – he was very grand, Lord of the Manor. But he was generous to the people of Minchinhampton.

I can remember on Sundays, I used to watch my grandmother baking. In those days, the fats were different – she used lard to make pastry and tarts. If I behaved myself, I'd end up with a slice of bread and lard. We put salt and pepper on it, and it was gorgeous. The lard was pure fat from the pig. We went the opposite to what you get told today. We had great big spotted dicks and suet puddings. Everything was full of fat.

We had one big living room and a pantry where I used to get my bread and lard. The pantry was always on the north side of houses where it was coolest. They would build in a marble slab to keep butter and such-like cold. Then there was the scullery where we did the washing. The boiler was like a fireplace with bricks and a big copper boiler inside. You not only washed the clothes in there, but you cooked your Christmas pudding inside it too!

May Vick (née Beard), born 1918

Dodging 'Bobby' Bourton

I was born at a little place at the top of a hill in Shortwood called The Fooks. There was a big house on the corner, which we thought of as a mansion in those days. We had an old two-up, two-down place. There was the kitchen, which was our living room, and a washhouse downstairs.

I was named Herbert after my father. He was going into the war, and my mother thought, 'This way we shall still have a Herbert Creed'. You just didn't know who would come back.

When I was a lad, I was chased by a policeman once for apple scrogging. I used to deliver the papers at Downend – that was the end of my round. Just over the wall was an orchard, and I saw these lovely apples. I was up a tree when I saw 'Bobby' Bourton standing on the other side. He dived over and started chasing me. I ran across the fields to Downend then I walked back up the same way and picked up my bike. The copper said to me, 'Did you see any lads running down the field?'

I said, 'No, I've just come up with the papers'. I walked up as if I'd been delivering all the time. It's not as if the apples were worth eating. They were sour old things, but I managed to get a couple in my pockets.

Herby Creed, born 1917

A boys' class in Minchinhampton from 1914. 'Gaffer' Perry is the teacher.

Fall from the Old Umbrella Tree

I am going to give it to you now straight from the horse's mouth, as the old saying goes. Firstly I went to Minchinhampton School when I was four year old. My teacher then was a Miss Ind which lived in West End, the shop we used to call Harmers Shop. From there the next place was the police station, which we all didn't look much forward to.

After we had twelve month in the infants, we did go from there down to Miss Hamlet. We had twelve month with Miss Hamlet, which was always a pleasure, especially on a Friday. She always used to send down to Mr Hughes and get about half a pound of sweets, and each one had two, some had three, in the afternoon just about playtime. Later on, we were shifted from that school up to the higher school, which we called the boys' school. The bell did ring at quarter to nine in the morning. We had to be in school by nine o'clock. We did leave at twelve. The school bell did ring again at quarter to two and from there, away we had to go until quarter past four. If there was any bad behaviour or discipline of any description, it was unpleasing to the teacher or to the school boss, 'Gaffer' Perry. You'd know what to expect. I only wish that discipline could be applied today. If you fooled about, you got a clout to the head or the cane.

The girls used to have a wifery where they used to do their cooking and washing.

From there I used to always look forward to the August holidays. As there was no other place like a playing field like people have got today, our playing field was The Park. That was a proper Godsend to us. Later on C.W. Jones used to rent The Park, and the horses, after they'd finished their day's work, were turned out in The Park –

and there was two or three cows. There was always a wall along the top of the park.

Most of the trees in The Park we used to name. There was the Old Umbrella, which I climbed one day, and there was a squirrel in the self-same tree, and I would test this squirrel out, and I fell. I come down on my hands. But here am I to tell you the story. Somebody came along and said, 'What's the matter?' and put me on a wheelbarrow and took me down home. Father's mother was in charge of us then. She said, 'Whatever's the matter now, then?' He said, 'George has been and fell down out of a tree in The Park'. 'Serve him right to do such a silly thing as that!' I had to wait 'til the doctor come. I said I wouldn't have the doctor. I couldn't stand it. Granny Ellins put on a bandage, and that was the end of that. I had a week from school, and it was misery when you had no-one to talk to nor nothing at all.

The outsiders used to visit Minchinhampton School, and one boy used to come from Avening. People do come from the Ragged Cot, Hampton Fields, Hyde, and Burleigh. Today they got to have transport. They never thought of having transport, because it wasn't knocking about in those days.

George Ellins, born 1897

Memories of Minchinhampton's Rector, Rex Hodson

The Rectory was the most wonderful childhood house. There was, because of my grandfather being not only Rector but an extremely athletic and attractive person as well, always something going on – someone coming or going, some interesting activity.

Every inch of the Minchinhampton School ground was used – this patch behind the old school was for growing vegetables.

He was a tremendous horseman and always delivered parish magazines on horseback – the stables were across the street from the house – and on hunting days he often took communion services with his boots and spurs plainly visible below his cassock.

In the attic was the most wonderful dressing-up box you can imagine – real, beautifully-made costumes for princesses and shepherdesses and kings and soldiers, including Turkish slippers and tin helmets from World War One, and a proper witch's hat with a raggedy cloak. We spent hours up there. If it was fine, we paraded round the garden in our finery; if wet, all round the huge house, including through grandfather's study. He never seemed to mind, though I imagine we exasperated those parishioners who had come to see him on deeply private business.

There were other charms beside the dressing-up box. One was a huge, beautiful old-fashioned rocking horse – dapple-grey, of course – and in the enormous icy bathroom there was a trapeze hanging from the cavernous ceiling. My uncles – David and Haro – could actually trapeze themselves into the vast, iron, claw-footed bath at the far end. We never dared.

There were also the hens. They were looked after by Dallow, the gardener, who managed to persuade me, when I was about four, that I had actually laid an egg. He made me squat down in the hen house and cluck madly, and then, in triumph, produced a warm speckled egg from the straw underneath me. It was far more of an accomplishment than writing novels, I can tell you.

It was also a house made for rituals. We always had breakfast in a little parlour that caught the morning sun (the sugar, brown and white, lived in little china houses whose roofs/lids lifted off); we always went across the Square for hot new rolls from the baker on Sunday mornings after church; we always – every holidays – made new tree houses along the yew tree walk at the top of the garden; we always made butter by shaking milk for not less than forever in jam jars; we always had to riddle out the Aga and carry huge craggy clinkers outside.

We were very, very lucky to have known the Rectory in what I am quite convinced was – thanks to my grandparents – its heyday.

Joanna Trollope, born 1943

A Cup of Well Water

It was a hard life when I was young, but you always had someone who would give you a hand. Everybody helped somebody else, and it was a lovely feeling. We lived in Newmarket, and Mrs Creed and her children lived near us up Bunting Hill. The baker wouldn't go all the way up there, so my mum used to take up her bread and milk every day. My mum was Florence Davis, and she nursed people and helped to deliver babies. Dad used to break in horses and do other bits and pieces for his work.

We had well water at our house, and it was beautiful. We'd lift the board on the bucket mum used to wind, and then we did sit on the step in the evenings and have a cup of it. That was all you wanted.

When I was four, I started at a little school in Shortwood for sixpence a week. It was run by Miss Wilkins, who used to rent the building from the chapel. She used to get up a concert every Christmas, and we did have it in front of the parents. We all dressed up.

The lovely, rolling green fields of Newmarket of yesteryear.

Then I went to the girls' school in Nailsworth by the church. I can remember we had Miss Drake, Miss Cooper, and our headmistress was Miss Brown. They were really happy days. Miss Brown used to cross her legs, and we could see the bottom of her long knickers when she did that. We used to think that was funny, but not unkindly.

I was good at sewing, and Lawyer Smith's mother used to present us with prizes. She lived in High Beeches. I was very good at hemming, and one year I was presented with a little chest of drawers, varnished and fancy down the front. I treasured it.

We walked from Newmarket to Nailsworth, then back to have lunch at home, and then on to school again. It didn't do us no harm. We played in the road with whip tops and marbles, and a big skipping rope. We played paper chasing up in Newmarket. You'd tear up pieces of paper and run where you wanted to, and the other children had to chase you. We'd go all round Bunting Hill. I used to play with Raymond Stevens and his brother Lewis, and Betty and Vera.

We'd play a lot with the water streams. Mrs Bevans grew watercress just below Jenners Farm. Everyone would go and buy some – it was only for coppers.

Muriel Newman (née Davis), born 1916

Always Tell the Truth

I was born in a churchyard, in Minchinhampton, but don't get me wrong! I was born in Church Cottage in the churchyard. That sounds a little bit better! It's known as Vestry Cottage now. Dr Brown brought me into the world. I was the sixth of seven children, and, when I was born, my father was reported to have said in broad

Gloucestershire, 'Ain't 'er lovely! I would like a laneful like 'er'. When I grew older, I was told about this and I said to him, 'I hope you don't mean Half Mile Lane, Daddy!'

Dr Brown was lovely – a plain man to look at. He must have been owed thousands of pounds in money. There was no National Health, but he still treated people, and very often he wouldn't even send the bill. He lived at the top of Tetbury Street, and had his surgery in a kind of a garage before he moved to Dr Brown's Road.

My father was the verger, and he used to have to unlock the church at seven each morning, then climb up the tower and ring the bell at eight o'clock for Holy Communion.

Jessie Kirby, aged three-and-a-half.

Victor Kirby aged twelve in 1887. He went on to become verger of Minchinhampton.

The first rector I remember was Canon Sears. He was a lovely gentleman – very musical with a beautiful singing voice. Of course, rectors were a little more aloof in those days. My sister, Eva, could remember one of the rectors' daughters getting married. The children of the village had baskets of rose petals, and they stood down Butt Street throwing them at the bride.

My parents were wonderful, old-fashioned parents. My mother would read us stories every night – and they always had a moral. I remember one she used to read called 'Froggy's Little Brother'. It was about a boy in the slums who nursed his sick brother. We all used to cry when she told us that one.

My mother used to say we must always tell the truth. I remember I would ask her, 'Is my neck clean?' and she used to say, 'Have you washed it?' Well, she always told us to say the truth, so I had to tell her I hadn't!

I went to school in Minchinhampton in the days when that was a lovely Cotswold stone building with a bell tower. I remember the smell of the coke stoves in the classrooms. There were children from Box and Hyde and Hampton Fields and Burleigh, and those children had to walk – all winds and weathers, they had to walk.

We had standards, not classes, and the standards went up from one to seven. And when you got to seven, and you were a little bit clever, you went into an extra class, and that was called X-seven. We had the normal lessons, mainly scripture, lessons taught us right from the Bible. We were taught the three 'R's. I think that is the base of all good teaching. We were taught certain handicrafts – how to hem properly, and darn, and knit and do all the various fancy stitches – featherstitch and herringbone – the real rudiments of ordinary knowledge. When it came to break time, this, in my day, was called playtime. And we didn't do sports or athletics. We used to call it drill and races.

When I was quite young, in the infants' school and the headmistress was Miss Hamlet, I remember her beautiful laugh, and also her beautiful hair. It was a lovely shade of grey, and it was quite an understood thing that she didn't wash it very often, but she used to brush it or rub it with a pure silk handkerchief. And I should say that was better than all the modern shampoos.

When I was in Miss Hamlet's class, we used to save a penny a week, and buy a postage stamp. It was either red or pink and this would go on a form on which there were twelve squares. When we got this form full, we took it to the post office and opened a post office bank account with one shilling.

One of the great days in the school life was May 24. I reckon there's hardly a child at school today who could tell us what May 24 is. Well, when I was at school it was and still is, in my mind, Empire Day. And on that day we used to all congregate in the playground, and the Union Jack was hoisted. And we all stood around this flag and we sang a song. I can't remember all of it, but two lines I do remember. These two lines were to the flag – 'We salute thee and we say, bless, Oh Lord, our

Jessie Kirby's mother, Sarah (known as Annie) Flooks, aged twelve, in 1887.

Norman Vick (middle row, third from left) in the 1930s, playing for Horsley British Legion Football Team, Stroud League third division.

land today'. And after that, we were all given an orange, and sent home for the rest of the day.

Jessie Kirby, born 1909

Keeping Pigs

Besides working 12 hours a day, father kept about 20 pigs. He would bring the pigs up to about 15 score (a score being 20 pounds) when they were so fat they couldn't run. I had to clean the pigs out every night when I came home from school, from the age of 10

onwards. I used a brush and a shovel. I had to feed the pigs after I had mucked them out. I'd go along the fields with two sack bags, and I had to pick dandelions, cow parsley and clover and give the pigs a bag of this to eat for their green stuff. It took me a couple of hours to do all that.

All the pig muck would be swept into a big heap outside the sty and, every three months or so, we'd borrow a horse and cart to take it up and put it on the allotment.

Father used to kill two pigs a year, one at one time and one at another. The rest went to a bacon factory owned by Porky – that's Teddy – Smith. He had a little factory at

The Cross in Nailsworth in a courtyard with a blacksmith's.

We'd kill the pigs by putting a noose around their nose, and I'd pull on it so they couldn't get away. Then we'd hold them down on a box in the garden, and a special bloke who was licensed to kill pigs – Nat Walkley – would kill them with a knife. That kept us in meat during the winter.

We'd cure the pigs in the Yew Tree. Saltpetre and brown sugar were rubbed on the side of the pig, then it would be turned over and more rubbed in the other side, and that would be done for nine months. When our mum wanted bacon, dad would go out and cut it. She would put it in a frying pan without any fat, and by the time she'd finished cooking, the frying pan was full of fat. It tasted lovely.

When the pig was dead on the box, Nat Walkley, would cut the belly open and get out all the heart and liver and kidneys, and we'd keep all that. Then we'd put the chitterlings in a tin bath and trot down the lane towards Binley Farm. There were springs of water there that came out of the bank, and we'd put a stick in the bank so that the water would run down it. You'd run the chitterlings up and down the stick to get them clean. Then we used to put them back in the bath and take them home. Mother would get the copper going and cook them. Then we'd eat them cold in sandwiches or hot with other food. They were a bit bland, but we were brought up on it.

Horsley village.

Vera Harvey's mother, Ethel (second row, third from left) in Minchinhampton infants' class of 1907. Her brother, Harold, is just below her.

We ate the trotters and the tail, and made a stew with the backbone. When the head was cooked, all the meat would drop off, and mother would make brawn by pressing it between two plates.

Norman Vick, born 1914

Miss Webb, I Be Afraid of Thee

Children from Nailsworth would go up to Minchinhampton School because it was such a good school. There were a few still in my mother's time, but probably more in her mother's time. They came on a Monday, and went back home on a Friday, and probably lodged with teachers. After all, the teachers were mostly 'misses'. Miss Webb taught my mother. She was head of the girls' school. Some of the boys thought a woman teacher was 'not on', but Miss Webb was a teacher who 'Would Be Obeyed'! Because this letter was about Miss Webb, my mother cut it out of the *Stroud Journal* a long time ago.

Dear Sir,

I wish that the Home Secretary had been at Hampton School in 1894, when the following episode took place and, to my mind, emphasises the value of control.

The schoolmaster was called away to Exeter for three days owing to the death of his father, and had left the control of his school during his absence to Miss Webb, the headmistress of the girls' school next door. One of the boys, aged eleven, was the terror of the younger ones and the despair of the headmaster. So when Miss Webb took over, he started to walk round punching other boys. His name was Evans.

Miss Webb: 'Evans, sit down in your seat at once.'
Evans: 'I shant cos I beant afraid of thee.'
Miss Webb: 'What did you say, Evans?'
Evans: 'I beant afraid of thee.'
Miss Webb was out of her desk like a shot and marched around the class to where Evans was shouting defiance. She grabs him by both ears and puts him on to her desk and, in full view of the class, tans his bare rump until it was the same colour of the red flannel shirt he was wearing.
He doesn't cry, but he mutters 'Please, Miss Webb. I be afraid of thee, Miss Webb.'
Miss Webb: 'That is better. Now go round to your seat and sit down.'
He went to his seat, but did not sit down.
Miss Webb: 'Evans, sit down!'
Evans: 'Please Miss, I can't sit down, but I be afraid of thee.'

I met Evans much later in life and I asked him if he remembered it. 'Yes', he said, and it was the best thing that had happened in his life.

Vera Harvey (née Smith), born 1934

Mr and Mrs Tombs, on Mr Tombs's retirement. Sadly, Charlie Tombs died soon after.

A Lesson in Life

Charlie Tombs was a wonderful long-time teacher at Minchinhampton School, under the headship of F.T. Robinson, 'Gaffer' to us boys.

Charlie used to tell us rather risqué stories, and I remember one about a fellow who went down the Niagara Falls in a barrel. Unfortunately, there was a nail sticking out of this barrel, and the chap hurt himself in a rather nasty place. Well, when the girls' school and the boys' school combined, Charlie was in a bit of a fix, because he couldn't tell these stories any more! I have to say, though, that they always had some sort of a point to them – a moral.

Charlie sat in front of his class at a trestle table. Sometimes the class showed signs of being unruly, but one snap of his fingers ensured dead silence. On one occasion, Charlie had set an arithmetic exam and, luckily, I was top in the test. He called me out to the front of the class, ceremoniously congratulated me, and shook my hand. As I turned to return to my seat, he booted me up the backside. I stopped and turned round in amazement, whereupon he quietly said, 'That, Alan, was to bring you back to size'. I have never forgotten that lesson, so ably applied.

Alan Hughes, born 1922

Dead Man Alive

I didn't like school much. Everyone went at three years old, full time, if your parents wanted you to. I remember Empire Day – 24 May. That was one of my first disappointments. All the school had to

Robert and Ruby Hughes, with sons Robert and Alan (right).

assemble outside on a patch of grass, and we used to sing *Rule Britannia* and *Land of Hope and Glory*. After you had done all the singing, the young ones would get a bun and the older classes would get an orange. After that, we had a half-day. I was longing for the day I got an orange, but the year before I was due, the school joined up and the headmaster stopped the buns and the oranges.

Before the school joined, the boys were in one half, and the girls in the other. We didn't dare fraternize with each other. The whole school used to go to church a lot more. We went every morning in Holy

Week, and Ash Wednesday, and other days like that.

One of my best friends was May Glastonbury who lived in Parsons Court. We played a fabulous game in the playground called Dead Man Alive. There were two teams and one would go off and hide. The other would gather coats, then so many would lay down on the ground with coats over them. The first team had to guess who was under the coats by feeling them.

I can remember going to London Zoo with the school. We went on the train for about half a crown. You didn't walk around the zoo – I think we were driven round in a little grey bus. We saved all year for the trip – our parents had to give us tuppence a week, which we took to the school to put into a fund.

You didn't move from the school until you were fourteen, unless you passed for the High School. If you went there, you had to walk to Brimscombe Corner and get the rail car to Stroud.

Ours has been a wonderful life. We almost saw the coming of the motorcars, and we certainly saw the coming of aeroplanes. I got sent in from school once. In those days, you didn't really ever see aeroplanes. We used to have to stand in two lines going in from playtime, and this one day we heard an aeroplane – and I looked up. I had to stay behind after school and write 'I must not look at aeroplanes when I am standing in line'.

May Vick (née Beard), born 1918

Dorothy Blair as a child, with her brother, Peter.

Dorothy's father, Randolph Bruton, used this building as his office. It's now a baker's.

Watching the Blacksmith

When I was a little girl, Brutons Ironmonger was where the Mad Hatter restaurant is now, and we lived next door. I had two brothers and two sisters, and an older half-brother, Peter. My father had first married a lady from Bristol, who had lost a husband who was a soldier. She died in childbirth, so Peter never knew his mother. My father remarried three years later.

I was nine or ten before I knew Peter wasn't my full brother. In those days, it never came up in conversation. I remember as plain as day going into Davis's, and a lady saying to me, 'Well, Peter isn't your real brother'. I rushed home saying, 'He is my real brother!' Then my mum explained all about it.

When we were children, there were a blacksmith, a farrier and a tinsmith working for Brutons. I believe the blacksmith's shop was on the site of two old cottages made into one, which was called The Corner of Market Street. When I knew it, it was just called The Yard. Further up The Yard, there was a carpenter's shop and a coach paint shop, and my father ran the whole caboodle by himself – his brothers had gone to South Africa.

I used to spend hours in the blacksmith's, watching them make horseshoes and bits of fences. It was dirty and smelly and, of course, we were forbidden to go in there – the language was a bit blue – but it was fascinating for children. The blacksmith, Mr Charles, allowed us to push the bellows to blow the fire up. The chap who did all the shoeing was Mr Burge, and the tinsmith was Snuffer Dangerfield. He was a tiny little man.

The blacksmith also made iron hoops for boys to play with, and we used to bowl the hoops down The Yard, and ride our tricycles.

There were seasonal games – sometimes marbles were in fashion, sometimes spinning tops or skipping and ball games. I can also vaguely remember being taken down to the mill-pond, which used to be by Davis's Mill, and seeing people skating on there.

When it was time for me to go to school, I started at a tiny private place at the house called Clovelly, in Northfields Road. The classroom was a little wooden hut in the garden. Miss Leonard ran it – she lived in the house with her parents. She was very tall and dark, and she had her hair in buns like earphones at the side of her head. When the school closed, she taught dancing in the rooms above the Social Club in Brewery Lane. I was quite young when I started – about four – because I used to cry to be allowed to go with my brother who was there.

I moved to Nailsworth Church School when I was seven. The headmistress, who was quite a disciplinarian, was Miss Brown. The first class I went into was Miss Drake's. She lived along the Bristol Road. Miss Cooper was another teacher, who was very tall and very strict. She used to teach sewing and, if your stitches were minutely too big, you had to take them out and start again. We were taught how to knit, and how to make socks.

Dorothy Blair (née Bruton), born 1921

Mother's Gunpowder Remedy

My mother had remedies if you were ill. When I was in my 'teens', I was having sties in my eyes and boils, so she said I had to have the treatment. She bought gunpowder from the chemist in Nailsworth, and she sprinkled it on the top of the milk. It wasn't very nice, but it purified the blood.

Stinging nettles were another cure. My mum would pick them and put them in a bag – it should be paper, not plastic. She'd pick the tops out, wash them thoroughly in a bowl of clean water, then squeeze them out. Then they would be boiled in a saucepan with clean water, and you'd drink that. That was good for the blood, too.

She was all for herbs – elderflower is another wonderful herb. And my mum made wine from cowslips. She was an old-fashioned lady.

I only went to the doctor's once until the time I was married. Dr Bletchley and Dr Wilson used to be at what is now Abbeyfields. They had a lady like a chemist in there and she would give you what the doctor said you had to have.

Muriel Newman (née Davis), born 1916

Playing Consequences with the Servants

Everybody had maids in those days. Dulcie Welham was one maid – she was my granny's lady's maid, and she was a dear. Ethel Head was another of my granny's personal maids. Granny's maids were healthy, high-spirited young girls who enjoyed life. They were never too busy to be sweet to a child. We used to have wild goose chases round Christowe garden. We were free to run round as long as we didn't go on the tennis court or the croquet lawn.

Florence was the parlour maid, and she waited at table, and answered the door, and brought people through. She'd also clean the silver and look after the dining room and the drawing room. I always ate with my

Mr and Mrs Woollcombe-Boyce, Anne's grandparents, who lived at Christowe.

grandfather and nanny in the dining room. I expect Nanny would eat her evening meal with the servants. My grandfather would always say Grace. He always had morning prayers after breakfast. Nanny and I attended those with the maids and anyone else staying in the house.

Lucy was the housemaid, and she would make the beds and clean the bathrooms and bring any invalids breakfast in bed.

Eva Kirby was a cook at one time, and Maggie Ponting followed. Dick Ponting was gardener, and Bailey was the chauffeur and looked after the electric light dynamo. I hated that thing because it chugged away and scared me rigid.

I was always accompanied by my mother or my nanny. Nanny would have been on a par with the parlour maid. She was called Maud Edwards and had been recommended by an old servant of Granny Playne's.

I used to like feeding the hens and collecting the eggs. Once I very proudly brought in the china eggs, and I was told very gently that those were for the hens to play with.

On a wet afternoon, we would play Consequences. Between two and three in the afternoon, the servants had time off, and sometimes, if it was wet, I would go and play with them. You played Consequences like this: you started off by writing down something like 'Albert Smith met…', then you'd write a girl's name, where they met, what they were doing, what he said to her and she said to him, and the consequence. The last bit was always, 'And the world said…'

I especially loved going down to Mrs Orpe's sweet shop. There were pink and white sugar mice with a string tail. You always bit the

Above left: *Anne Woollcombe-Boyce, as a young child, on the Long Walk at Springfield.*
Above: *Mrs Edward Playne, Anne Woollcombe-Boyce's maternal grandmother, at Springfield.*

Left: *One of the first cars in Minchinhampton, belonging to the Woollcombe-Boyce family, with the chauffeur, probably a Mr Bailey.*

head off first, then carried on down until only the tail was left. Then there were jelly babies, liquorice braid, liquorice pipes, and sherbet in little bags with a ring round the neck, which you could wear afterwards. You used a liquorice tube to suck up sherbet through. There were flat sweets with mottoes on them, bulls eyes and humbugs. The hard sweets were kept at the back in big glass jars.

There were gob stoppers about the size of a pingpong ball. After you had sucked them for a bit, you pulled them out of your mouth and they had changed colour – brown, green, yellow. They went down like that until you got to a tiny ball, then you'd crunch it.

Coming out of the shop with a gob stopper in your cheek, you'd very likely meet a stately acquaintance of your grandmother's. Nanny would say, 'Take it out and put it into your handkerchief!' Well, your handkerchief lived in your knickers because there would be no pockets in your dresses, so you'd get it out, put in your gob stopper and stuff it back up your knickers.

Mrs Orpe couldn't have been more than in her sixties because her hair was still brown. She had it in a tight knot at the back of her head, and her face was round like a rosy, wrinkled apple. She dressed in a long dark skirt, sometimes with an apron, and a dark blouse buttoned right up to her neck, as if she'd been frozen in time since 1900.

Anne Woollcombe-Boyce, born 1921

'Poshy' Orpe

The shop that was the most popular with the children was Mrs Orpe's. We used to say, 'I'm going up to Orpe's'. Now her shop was opposite The Swan on the corner where you go up to Park Farm Court. I don't know what her husband's name was, but he was always known as 'Poshy' – I think because he came from London and he brought the word 'posh' with him. Mrs Orpe was a little rotund lady. I shouldn't think she was any more than 5ft tall. And we used to go in with our ha'pennies or pennies and say, 'I want a pennyworth of sweets, and please may I have a look round?' Mrs Orpe used to pick us up, all 5ft of her, and we used to see the wonders of her sweet shop. There were sherbet dabs – that's a little paper bag with some sherbet in, and a dab of toffee on a stick. You'd dip the toffee in, then lick the sherbet off. There were also sherbet suckers, which were similar, except you had a piece of tubular liquorice, which you sucked up, and up came the sherbet. It came up into your mouth and down through your nose if you weren't careful.

I think we nearly always bought popcorns. They were very much like breakfast cereal, all covered in sugar. We bought those mainly because they were very very light, and we got ever such a lot for our money. Comfits, we used to buy. They had little love messages on, and heart shapes and liquorice … Liquorice was lovely. We used to buy liquorice pipes that we pretended to smoke, and liquorice shoelaces. This was like rib liquorice about half an inch to an inch wide, and we used strip off these little narrow flakings of liquorice, of course, to make it go all the much farther.

Jessie Kirby, born 1909

Doing the Errands

When I was about ten or eleven, I would go over to the railway, train spotting. All the Midland trains used to use the branch. We went down on to the platform and played with the railway men's children. Mr

A chess match between Ron Woodward (left) and Bob Mills, presided over by classmates, and the headmaster of the British School, Mr T.H. Wallis. The year was 1931.

A photograph of boys from Nailsworth's British School, date unknown.

Hopkins was the first stationmaster I remember. Then there was Mr Faulkner. He used to do recitations and sing. He used to look after Woodchester station as well as Nailsworth. He went up and down between them on his bike. That would be in the 1930s.

I used to have to go down to the goods yard with a wheelbarrow to take empty drums that grandfather wanted sent back to Bristol. The drums had been used to make paint up for our business. Our business was originally a carpenter's and undertaker's that was run by my great great grandfather. We found a receipt from 1840, but it may go back even further than that.

I used to have to sweep up all the shavings in the workshop from when I was old enough to hold a brush. Grandfather sharpened all the tools on the grindstone, and I would have to turn it round and round, sometimes for an hour or more. I didn't mind. I would be about ten years old, then.

I remember going to the Shears in Watledge when it was a pub, with a shilling, and I'd buy a pint of beer and an ounce of tobacco for my grandfather. They didn't mind me buying beer – they knew who it was for. I'd go with a jug for them to fill up.

Ron Woodward, born 1921

Mr Yeo and the Sausages

My mother was brought up here, and her mother and father owned Box House. Her first cousin, Mabel, was the daughter of Mr Bryans, the Rector. She married Herbert Playne who came to inherit Springfield. The Playnes had been 200 years in this area. One branch owned Longfords Mill, and the other branch owned a brewery. Ted Playne, Beatrice Playne's brother, told me once that Springfield House was built from the profits of the brewery.

Mother was Mary Paolina Hill, and she was very devoted to Box. She started the WI in Box after the war. We lived in London and used to come here for holidays. To begin with, Mother used to rent houses. Then she had what is now called St Davids built by Simmonds. It was a holiday home for the children. It had central heating, a double garage, a fridge and a sink.

Mother had a car – MU162 – which she used to drive. We'd come here from London along the Great West Road, which took hours because of delivery vans and traffic lights. We'd have a picnic on the way. There were two ways you could go – one was through Maidenhead.

We loved to go wild in Box Woods and Gatcombe Woods. They were full of primroses, bluebells and kingcups. We were quite free to wander in Gatcombe Woods. Colonel Ricardo was terribly nice. I remember having to dress up to go to tea with him once.

Everything was far less supervised – we used to light fires in the woods and cook sausages over them! We'd go down the field next to the church in Box, over the stream and on to an island where we made an encampment. Mr Yeo, the manager of Longfords Mill, used to live in Hope Cottage by the church in Box. A married couple called Stubberfield lived with him – he was the chauffeur and she was his housekeeper. Mr Yeo was very fat and unmarried, but he was quite interested in this awful pack of children living near him. One day we said he would get a nice meal if he came with us to the woods. He came down and we cooked him sausages! He was a lonely old man really, and very kind. He walked down to the mill every day through the slim-slams – I think they're really called kissing gates – with his dog, a black Labrador.

Mother had some extraordinary ideas – she was all for the latest things. The fashion at one time was to have your tonsils out. I remember her lining three of us up at once. The consultant came and took all our tonsils and adenoids out on the kitchen table. I can remember my throat being very sore!

Another of her ideas was that we must know the English countryside. She took the Long Cottage in Box, opposite the church – which was a tin one then – and rented that for the summer. She left us in the charge of vague governesses. There was a gas mains being laid in the road outside, and the men set up a camp we used to go in. We'd talk to them for hours, and no-one seemed to mind.

Box Farm, which is now a house, was a working farm then with corn and milk. The farmer, Mr Chamberlain, used to do a milk round with a great big can, which he carried from house to house. He ran the farm with his son Arthur who had a deformed hand. They taught us to milk by hand, and we did the harvest. They did a crop rotation, and every so often there would be wheat growing that had to be swapped. We had to help with that. It would be brought in by cart, and we'd get a ride on it afterwards.

Lady Mary Rawlinson (née Hill), born 1923

Box Farm, with Arthur Chamberlain, his father Albert, and farmhand Walter, Lady Mary Rawlinson, and her sister Sara on the hay wagon.

Children playing round a maypole in Box.

Stuck up the War Memorial

I was born in Woefuldane Farm – there are many legends about where the name comes from. When we were young, we were told that the dips at the farm are where all the blood ran when the Danes and the Saxons were fighting there.

My parents had eleven children, though one of them, Mary, was knocked down and killed by a motorbike when she was five, coming home from Sunday School. I've got all the articles from the *Stroud News and Journal* about it.

I was number eight, and there were five girls and six boys. Nurse Burton delivered all my mother's children, except the last one who she had in hospital. After him, the doctor told my mother, 'No more!'

Nurse Burton lived in Tetbury Street, and she used to bicycle everywhere. She was lovely.

My mother had no help at home, and she was more often than not out in the fields helping my father. But she was always there for us when we got up and when we got home from school.

I'll always remember the great big long table we used to sit around. My mother kept a long stick in the middle to give us a rap on the knuckles if we talked – we were never allowed to speak at the table.

My father used to make all our bread. In the back kitchen there was a big baker's oven with a fire underneath. The flour came in big barrels, and my father put the dough in the oven with a large shovel. It used to smell lovely. We hardly ever saw

Sheila's hard-working mother, Maud Smith, with eight of her eleven children.

my father. He had to go out before it was light and came back when the younger children were in bed.

Fridays or Saturdays were bath time. A big tin bath was put in front of the fire, and we'd have to get in, one after the other. The first-born was the last in.

We walked to school – about a mile, but it seemed a lot longer when we were small. The bigger ones used to take the smaller ones. I did enjoy school. We took our own sandwiches. If we had a cow calved down and there was a lot of milk, my mother made loads of individual rice puddings.

I can remember the head, Mr Robinson, calling out the names of any naughty boys in assembly. They had to hold their hands out and the cane would go down on their fingers. You could see them wincing and tears spring in their eyes, but they'd never cry. Mr Tombs was another teacher – you

never saw him lose his temper. He and his wife used to live in Well Hill, and she was manageress of Walkers Stores where the estate agents is now.

The boys had one playground and the girls had the other. We played hopscotch and skipping. My brothers were kept home now and again. My father would do timber felling, and, if he had a big job on, he would keep the boys off school to help, though he wasn't supposed to.

I never saw it, but I was told once about a gang of boys – including my brothers – who climbed to the top of the War Memorial in the Market Place. PC Buckle came along and saw them, and told them to come down, but they wouldn't because they were too frightened. Of course, Mr Buckle knew all the children, so he told them, 'I'm going to stay here until you do come down'. In the end he threatened to

Woefuldane Farm.

Sheila Jarman's father, Joe Smith, with the family donkey.

go and get all their fathers. PC Buckle wasn't fierce to look at. He always seemed as if he had a smile on his face. But the boys knew they didn't have to be on the wrong side of him.

I had pneumonia and pleurisy when I was ten, and I stayed at home in bed. We were three to a room, and the other children had to move to another bedroom, and my mother slept with me. I remember, when I was ill, I had a nosebleed for about three hours. Dr Brown came along and told me that if it hadn't stopped when it did, I would have had to have gone to hospital.

Mary, my sister who was killed, had had scarlet fever when she was very little and she was taken to Standish Hospital. She was very upset because she and the brother above her, Peter, were inseparable, so they let him go in as well, and he stayed there. My mother and father weren't allowed to go and see her, because she would get so upset. So my father used to cycle there and look in through the window at her.

We only had the fire in the kitchen. We had another in the room that was kept for best, but we weren't allowed to go in there. My mother used to put bricks in the oven and wrap them up for the beds. But we didn't feel the cold because we had so many clothes to put on. You would have a vest, a Liberty bodice – like a waistcoat with rubber buttons – a jumper and a cardigan. My mother made most of our clothes, and they were all hand-me-downs. There was nothing new, but we were always clean and tidy.

If my mother ever did sit down, she was always doing something – sewing or such like.

Sheila Jarman (née Smith), born 1931

A Nice Little Bouquet

I was born in Parson's Court, which is now the car park. It was originally a mill – a very tall building. They turned it into three houses in a row, one in the corner with another at right angles. We had a cellar, one living room and a tiny kitchen-cum-pantry, a bedroom and a small box room, and another bedroom above that.

Dr Brown delivered my sister Poppy and me. We had a younger sister who died at five months of bronchial pneumonia. When she was born, she was a very weak baby.

Dr Brown named my older sister. She had red hair, and was born on Armistice Day, and Dr Brown said to my mother, 'You've got a lovely little Poppy'.

I was named Iris, and my little sister was Violet. Dr Brown told my mother 'You've got a nice little bouquet'. And she said, 'If you don't mind, I'll stop at a button hole!'

My mother told me that things went wrong when I was born. I was all soaped to be washed when they took one look at mother, threw me on the bed, and dealt with her instead.

I went to Minchinhampton School at the age of four. Miss Fassnidge was my teacher in the infants. The head was Miss Jukes who was rather strict. I got into trouble in her class. The lady who used to bring the pay, Miss Hamlet, called. We were supposed to be sitting quietly, but the lad behind me pinched my bottom. I jumped, and I was reprimanded severely and sent into Miss Fassnidge's class with the babies and made to sit at the back in disgrace. They were teaching us the nursery rhyme *Little Boy Blue* at the time. I can remember it to this day, and I was most annoyed because it wasn't my fault.

I remember we children used to do one

Miss Lewis's class, Standard IV at Minchinhampton School in 1939. Iris Dyer – then Ellins – is in the seated second row, fourth from the right.

potato, two potatoes, three potatoes, four. Five potatoes, six potatoes, seven potatoes, more. This game decided who was 'on it'. One person patted each hand, held out in front one at a time, and if your hand was 'more' you put it behind your back. This continued round and round until the last hand was left. We played hopscotch – both kinds, with six squares and with nine. And a whole lot of us used to play 'The big ship sailed on the Illey Alley Oh' Two people would make a bridge with their arms, and the rest of us went through. If you were going through at the end of the song, you were out.

Iris Dyer (née Ellins), born 1930

The Turmut Hower

My grandmother would sit and read stories to us – she did a wonderful Gloucestershire accent. The front room was the Sunday room, and on Sunday evenings we would go in for stories. She'd read one about Roger Plowman, who was a person from this area. He had a lady friend called 'Sairy Jane', and the stories were all about his adventures in London. This is part of what she would read:

Cook hed bin kindish, an' so I starts the ditty, "The Vly be on the Turmuts."

THE TURMUT HOWER

I be a turmut hower,
Vram Glo'stershire I came,
My parents be hard working volk,
Giles Wapshaw be my name.
The vly, the vly
The vly be on the turmut,
An' it be aal me eye, and no use to try,
To keep um off the turmut.

Zum be vond o' haymakin',
An zum be vond o' mowin'
But of aal the trades thet I likes best,
The vly, &c.

'Twas on a zummer marnin',
Aal at the brake o' day,
When I tuck up my turmut hower,
An' trudged it far away.
The vly, &c.

The vust place I got work at,
It was by the job,
But if I hed my chance agen,
I'd rather go to quod.
The vly, &c.

The next place I got work at,
'Twer by the day,
Vor one old varmer Vlower,
Who sed I wur a rippin turmut hower.
The vly, &c.

Zumtimes I be a mowin',
Zumtimes I be a plowin',
Getting the vurrows aal bright an' clear,
Aal ready vor turmut sowin'.
The vly, &c.

An' now my zong be ended,
I 'ope you wont call *encore*,
But if you'll kum here another night,
I'll seng it ye once more.
The vly, &c.

'Never heerd a better son in me life. We
must hev another, next time you drops in,
Roger', she sed.

Vera Harvey (née Smith), born 1934

Bill Perrett, first hand shop assistant, Mrs Tombs, Mrs Dolly Messenger, Mrs Stone, and Georgie Edmunds, in the 1940s.

Working at Walkers

I started at Walkers Stores in 1928 when I was fourteen. I went there straight from Stroud Central School, and I was there for forty-eight years. I got the job from Somerset. I was staying with my grandmother when her friend came to visit.

She said, 'I've got a sister who works in a shop in Minchinhampton. Her assistant is ill so she needs another one'.

The shop was very cold – there was no heating, or hot water, and just gas lighting. It was very hard work. We had to be there by half past eight in the morning, and we closed about seven at night, but I usually left

Georgie Edmunds on her BSA Bantum motorbike.

about half past eight. That was six days a week, and occasionally we went in on Sunday when we were stocktaking. I used to bike home to Avening. I got 10 shillings a week, but no concessions in the store. On Christmas Eve, we were open until eleven at night. One Christmas, I was cycling home with the errand boy from Cherington. We parted at Hampton Fields. The clock struck midnight, and I saw my father walking up the hill to see if I was all right. I must have been about eighteen.

People brought orders in on pieces of paper, and the errand boys would deliver the goods for free. The grand people would not come into the shop. We'd have to go out to them with a piece of paper and write their orders down, whether it was raining or not. One lady, a Miss Anderson who lived in Box, used to come on a horse, and we'd have to go out to her, too.

It was nerve-wracking for me when I started, though we never had awkward customers. The first lady I had to take an order from in the shop said to me, 'I'm Mrs Llewellyn'. She looked at me and said, 'You don't know how to spell that, do you?' I said, 'No!' so she spelt it for me. I've never forgotten how to spell that name!

There was the Co-op up West End, Harmers Stores, the Cross Stores, and Hughes Stores past the men's club – another old-fashioned grocer's like us. We all helped each other. If we ran out of anything, we'd run up to Mr Hughes and get it, and he'd come down to us. We'd write it all down on a piece of paper, and on Saturdays we'd settle up.

Mr Ogden owned the clothes shop on The Cross. He was a very nice man. He came round to Avening to collect money – people would pay on the 'never-never'.

On Whitsun the fair always came to Minchinhampton. They had no fridges, so I was sent up to knock on the caravan doors to see if they wanted an order. I was quite shy so I hated doing that. I did go into Miss Rogers's caravan once, who was the boss of the show. She had a beautiful caravan, with lovely brass, china and glass. It was spotlessly clean.

We used to get the gypsies around sometimes. They tried to sell us things like lace. They were quite all right. They camped in the Cherington Lanes.

I liked it when children came into the shop. We used to have a shelf of tins with glass lids by the counter, containing biscuits – Jacobs, H&Ps, Crawfords. We used to give the children biscuits when they came in. During the war, people like H&Ps would only make a few biscuits because they couldn't get the ingredients and they wanted to keep their standards up. But another company carried on making biscuits called 'Hiawatha', which were not very nice. Mr Tombs, the schoolteacher at Minchinhampton, was teaching the children at school the poem, *Hiawatha*. One little boy said, 'I don't mind learning about him, but I don't like his biscuits'!

Our manageress, Miss King, married Mr Tombs. He was a lovely man – so kind to everyone. He would speak to a tramp the same as anyone else. When he retired, they gave him a lovely chair as a leaving present, at the school. He died about a fortnight later. At his funeral, there was one little boy there who, of his own accord, raised his hand in salute and said, 'Goodbye, Sir'.

It was hard work in the war. Everything was rationed, and had to be weighed up. Cooking fat came in great big blocks and you used to have to cut it into two ounces. It was hard and it used to shoot everywhere when you cut it.

I became manageress just after the war, in 1946, when Mrs Tombs retired. I had a motorbike by then, which was quite unusual for a woman. Some people used to time themselves by it. One day, I didn't go to work until later in the day, and one person told me I'd made them late. They said, 'I was waiting for you to come past!' Mrs Enid Dallow put on a retirement party for me. She was so kind, and it was absolutely wonderful.

Georgie Edmunds, born 1914

Easy on the Horse

I remember the shop premises, run by my grandfather, Francis Charles Hughes, until his death in 1931. He had run the business since 1886, when he took over from his brother John James Hughes who, before him, had run the business since 1869. In 1931, my father took over the business.

My father told me that, prior to the First World War, he used to drive in a horse and trap, delivering groceries to houses and cottages, all the way to Oaksey. He would put up at the public house in that village, his horse being stalled at the rear, and travel back to Minchinhampton next day, calling at the same houses and cottages, collecting their orders for the following week.

I used to travel with him sometimes to Nailsworth railway station, to collect goods for the shop, which had arrived there. We always travelled via New Road, Forwood and Devil's Elbow because, on the way back, this route was less of a strain on the horse. I remember Jack, the horse, very well and, today, I've one of Jack's horseshoes nailed to the wooden wall of my shed.

Sometimes, on bank holidays, we would go in the horse and trap to Cirencester Park,

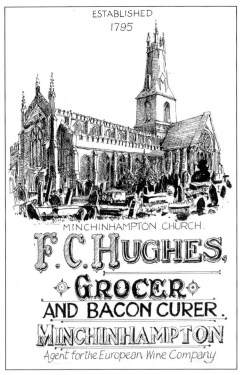

ESTABLISHED
1795

MINCHINHAMPTON CHURCH.

F. C. HUGHES,
GROCER
AND BACON CURER.
MINCHINHAMPTON
Agent for the European Wine Company

A poster for Hughes's grocery store.

The lids were made of glass. We used to buy broken biscuits from Mr Hughes because they were ever so much cheaper. Further on down the High Street, where Walkers Stores was, Mr Benjamin used to keep a grocer's shop there. He had an enormous red nose and, even to this day, I think of him as 'Cherry Nose' Benjamin. From him, we used to buy biscuits in the shape of letters. When we got them home, we used to try to make our names. We never could.

And then there was Viners, the chemist's shop. Originally, Mr Viner traded at a shop on the corner called The Cross Stores. He used to have a little hansom cab which he drove people about in. And Mrs Viner used to do the driving. Eventually he moved up to where the chemist is now. He made and patented some lemonade – Viner's Lemonade. It was lovely. Another thing he sold and recommended was a certain type of hair restorer. 'I can recommend it!' said Mr Viner, and, do you know, he was as bald as a coot himself! But he still recommended his hair restorer.

where we would play and picnic. This was the only holiday my father got until he closed the shop in 1943.

Alan Hughes, born 1922

A Yard of Hatty Lastic

I remember Hughes's shop. That was situated where Arden House is now. Incidentally, Arden House is one of the oldest, if not the oldest, house in Minchinhampton. That had a smell to it – it was coffee, and I don't know else. There were lovely mahogany counters in that shop, and, in front of the counter, there were stacked up huge 7lb biscuit tins, tilted at an angle so you could see their contents.

From Laits, the bakery, we used to buy lovely fruit cakes for sixpence. And then came Ogdens, a lovely shop. I can remember Miss Dowding serving in Ogdens' shop. In those days, the girls wore hats, winter and summer, even to school. We used to keep them on by a piece of elastic under our chin. And when this elastic broke, we were sent to Ogdens for some more. Well, I used to go in and say, 'I want a yard of hatty lastic'. And, do you know, for ages, I didn't realise that what I really wanted was hat elastic. Things were priced at ridiculous prices by today's standards. But if anything cost elevenpence three farthings, or one and elevenpence three farthings, we didn't get a farthing change, but we had a packet of pins instead.

An early view of Minchinhampton's High Street, showing a sweet shop run by a Mrs Critchley.

I can remember the last lamp lighter, and he was called Percy Grange. Hampton used to be lit by gas lamps on a pilot. Percy Grange would come along with a long stick with a hook at the end. He'd put his hook in the chain hanging from the lamp, pull it down, and the light would come on. He was a little man who lived in Parson's Court. Grange Close is named after him.

When I left school, I worked in a shop in Well Hill called Close and Redman, which sold haberdashery and gentleman's things. Mr Close used to measure gentlemen for suits, which were very likely made at Hill Paul's. He sold ladies' underwear, and lace and elastic. He was an excellent pianist, and he and his friends had a little dance band – Premier Dance Band – which would play for the dances.

I wasn't allowed to go to a dance unless one of my brothers went. We used to have Flannel Dances in the Market House where the men wore casual clothes. There was always an annual dance in aid of the Nurses' Association, when Dr Brown and Nurse Burton started off the dancing together.

Jessie Kirby, born 1909

In for a Penny

There was a little shop in West End run by a Mrs Essex. In our silly brains, she was an elderly lady and we thought she was a bit odd. She sold sweets, and ice cream which she made herself. We would find a packet of ten Woodbines in the street and we'd get out the silver paper. Then we would get our penny and wrap the silver paper round it. We would smooth it and smooth it until it would look to us like a half crown. Then we'd troop up to Mrs Essex to buy a pennyworth of sweets, thinking we would get a half crown's worth of change. She would take this "half crown" and look at it, then look at us. Slowly she'd peel the silver paper off, and she'd never say a word. I graduated with my pocket money from a penny a week, to a penny on a Friday and a ha'penny on a Wednesday.

May Vick (née Beard), born 1918

Rubbish Through the Trap Door

Father used to run a little fish stall in Market Street, Nailsworth. I remember when I was a boy, he used to send to Grimsby for fish on the Nailsworth train. It would come packed in ice. I would go down to the station and pick it up – I always had to get a receipt. I'd put the fish on my father's bike, between the pedals, because he didn't have a carrier bike.

Dad was very fussy about his appearance. He was crazy about hygiene, which wasn't easy in those days because there were no taps or hot water, and he brought me up the same. You couldn't say he was well dressed because he didn't have the money, but he was always smart. Even when he was threadbare, he'd have a shine on his shoes like the sun.

To get water, I had to go down six or seven hundred yards to a little place where there was a tap with spring water. You had to push a handle to get it out. That was a daily job. We had a barrel catching rainwater outside the house. Everyone had one of those – they were essential. That water was used for all our washing.

Father came out of the Great War disabled. It was something to do with gas that gave him breathing problems, but he got better over the years. Because he wasn't able to carry on with his normal living, they gave him a lump sum, and a pension of ten shillings per week. He used that to start up a shoemaker's business. He repaired and sold shoes. He got them from a firm in Bristol. We had two little shops in Nailsworth, one in Market Street and one where William's Kitchen is now. The William's Kitchen shop had a brook flowing under it. We had a trap door over it, and we'd throw the rubbish straight in there. When they repainted that shop about fifteen years ago, they found my father's name still underneath.

My sister Gwen used to sit up at Fooks with a box of laces pretending to run a shop like Dad. One day, one of the gentry came by on his horse and actually bought a pair of laces. Gwen was thrilled to bits.

There were seven children in our family: Evelyn, Winifred – both of them died in childbirth in their twenties – Stella, Gwen, Phyllis, me, and Raymond.

In Nailsworth, they used to sell off meat cheap on a Saturday night because, of course, there were no fridges, and mother used to wait until then to buy. There was no problem with not having a fridge in our house – with seven children, food never hung about!

The shops would stay open until seven or eight o'clock when they had stock to get rid of. They would be lit by paraffin lamps, which gave out a brilliant light. But they made a funny fizzing noise.

Herby Creed, born 1917

'Poor Horses'

Every evening, at about five o'clock, the coal carts would come up Well Hill from

Nailsworth. The yard was at Park Farm, and we always said 'Poor horses!' because of the huge lorries they had to pull. We used to stand out because the coal lumps would fall off the back of the carts, and we'd quickly pick them up. We'd buy coal from an old lady called Mrs Boulton who lived with her son 'Leggy' in the house between the two roads that looks down West End. She had great big scales with a platform where she would weigh out one hundred weight of coal. I think that cost about two shillings.

We had no dustbin lorries then. All of us down Well Hill had handcarts and, on Saturdays, we children had to take the rubbish to the tip, which was halfway down on the right hand side of New Road.

Down Well Hill, there's King's Street and up there, there's two spouts – two pipes coming out of the wall. That's all the water we had for bathing and washing. In our kitchen, we used to have a pump. If you had rain, you got a bit of water in the pump, but it wasn't anything much. There was a stream down the side of Well Hill that produced something like clay. We children used to get this clay and make cups and saucers and dry them in the sun.

May Vick (née Beard), born 1918

Monday Was Washday

I was born in a three-bedroomed cottage in Burleigh, and I was the last of five children – one girl and four boys. I can remember washday quite clearly – everything needed ironing. Mother had two flat irons, which she heated on the fire. She used one while the other was getting hot. Monday was the washday whether it was wet, or deep in snow. If it was raining, it was a pain because we only used to have the one fire, so all the washing was hung around it. Then the dirty water was thrown over the garden.

We had no gas, no electricity, no sewerage, no bathroom. All we had was a tap, which came through the wall and dripped into a basin on the bench. But that was a luxury because our neighbours had a standpipe, which they shared, which froze in the winter. Some people used the spring water, and they used to walk a long way with two buckets on a yoke over their shoulder.

For lighting, we had a paraffin lamp which dad hung from the ceiling because that was a safer place to put it.

Stan Dyer, born 1925

White Washing

There was a young woman down in the village, doing some washing on washday. And there were some men working near the cottage, doing some jobs. The woman put out the washing, and one of the workmen called out, 'What have you done with all that washing, Missus? You've washed all the white out!' Well, there wasn't any Daz in those days!

Vera Harvey (née Smith), born 1934

A Town Guide to the Past

I can tell you many changes. Minchinhampton had about six streets in those days – nine public houses in those streets too. No outside houses – the only outside house was Barcelona Farm in the Windmill Road, and Windmill House. In Dr Brown's Road, there were no houses at all.

At the Blue Boys, there was Miss Beale's house, the farm, and Mr Edgar Evan's house. Down the Butt Street, there were no houses on the right hand side until you got to The Coigne where opposite is three cottages.

Where the car park is were two cottages, which you entered through an archway, which was called the Hole in the Wall. Friday Street, was practically the same as now. On the Tetbury Road, at Woefuldane, there was a small cottage with a very large garden where we bought fruit and vegetables. Down Tetbury Street was Mr Jefferies, cabinet maker, Mr Hall, the baker, and a blacksmith's forge. Up the West End, there was a slaughter house, between Mr Taylor's and Mr Doel's paper shop. And opposite was the almshouse, which was given by Colonel Ricardo many years ago to accommodate eight elderly women of Minchinhampton. There were eight rooms in the house, and they each had one room, very comfortable. On the corner of Box Lane, there was a Miss Boulton who used to sell coal from that yard.

In Park Farm, the horses and coal carts were kept, belonging to Mr C.W. Jones. They used to go to Nailsworth to bring up the coal every morning, and we bought it at eighteen shillings a ton, summer prices. Down the Well Hill, was another blacksmith's forge. At the bottom of The Shard was a farmhouse where we used to be able to buy milk, skimmed milk, at a penny a quart.

Dr Brown's house was the first to be built in Dr Brown's Road. It was built on what was originally called the Camp Field where we used to play games. Years before my time, my uncle told me told me the soldiers used to be billeted there at intervals. The Park was a lovely park, surrounded by a high wall with an entrance gate by the church, and another one at the top of Besbury Lane, which went under an archway.

We have a most lovely church, not much alteration there really, just the porch room added on to the front. The Revd Bryans used to give some beautiful sermons. The church was always very full, and the bells used to ring out for the morning and evening services on Sundays. And very often the bell ringers would ring hymn tunes on the bells, which we all enjoyed very much.

Where the Memorial now stands, was a draper's shop owned by a Mr Thompson. When he left the shop, Mr Ogden took it on. He never made a success of it, and afterwards the Rector's wife, Mrs Bryans, bought it for a headquarters for a Boys' Brigade we had in mind. At the back of it was a room where the schoolgirls had cooking lessons.

We had a fire brigade. The engine was kept under the Market House. The horses were in The Park – it was drawn by horses in those days. When there was a fire, the church bell rang. But by the time the firemen had got out the engine and the horses from The Park, the fire was over. Very often, there was only a chimney on fire.

The baker's and confectioner was a Mr Close. Then The Priory was the doctor's house. Dr Faldo lived there at one time. We had two good doctors – a Dr Church, which lived at the Coigne, and Dr Faldo who eventually moved down to The Close. Good old family doctors, they were.

Where the Revd Davies lives, was a grocer's shop owned by Mr Hughes for many, many years. Where the club is was a chemist, a Mr Simpkins. A wonderful chemist too. He was a crippled man but he gave some very good medicines. He had good trade because you didn't go to the doctor every little thing – he had to be paid. We didn't have the money to pay doctors with, unless it was something very serious. Opposite was a shoe shop. Where Mr Dallow lived, of course, was a public house, the White Hart. In the olden days, long before my time, of course, it was an old coaching station. Next door lived Mr Orpe who used to let out horses and carriages – no motorcars in those days. Then there was Mr Ogden's shop where I worked for over thirty years. Prices were a little bit different in those days. I used to be able to sell men's socks 6d and 1s a pair; men's vests and pants, 1s 11½d; sheets, 6s 11d and 8s 11d; men's trousers, 8s 11d.

The rent of the cottages was about 2s 6d, and 3s a week. Of course, in those days not many people had gas. The cottages were lit with paraffin lamps. There was no water shortage – we had several wells, nearly one in every street, and also the spout at the bottom of the Well Hill, which was very useful. We used to have a farmer from outside come along the streets with wild rabbits at a shilling each. Fish came round the streets, cod at sixpence a pound, herrings three for sixpence.

There was no entertainment in Minchinhampton. We had to make our own entertainment by playing cards and singsongs in friends' houses. But occasionally, we had a concert in the Market House – all local talent. We had a wonderful comedian, a Mr E. Jones. He lived at Bank House, and was an uncle to Mr Jack Simmonds. He was a star, as they call them today. He used to keep the audience in fits of laughter.

I can tell you one funny story about a very old lady that lived near us in my young days. She was very fond of a little bit of gossip. It used to make us laugh. After she'd told you a tale, she always used to say, 'Well that's as it was told to I, so if it's a lie, well thee's gotten as good as I'. That's a little bit of broad Gloucester, isn't it?

Kitty Dowding, born 1884

The Park, before houses were built on the near side of Butt Street.

A portrait of Nailsworth.

Brown Paper Parcels, Tied Up With String

Most people shopped at the Co-op in Nailsworth, and my mum would go shopping every day. We had a 'divvy' – two shillings in the pound. You had a little chitty with a number on it and, when you'd bought what you wanted, the assistant wrote out the chitty. The funny thing was, the assistants would always know your number without you saying it.

Everything would be packed up in a brown paper parcel, tied up with string. Somehow, they would break the string with their hands – there must have been a knack to it.

Sugar was loose, and they scooped it up and put it in blue paper bags. Butter was sold in blocks on a marble top, and they cut off what you wanted and wrapped it in greaseproof paper. You kept your cold things on a slab in the pantry.

We got our clothes from Yarnolds. I didn't think we were terribly well off, but my mother used to give our old clothes to a family who lived up Tetbury Lane. Morris's was a draper's shop in George Street, next to the bank, which sold women's clothes. Mr Morris lived in a council house, and he was a jolly sort of chap. My mother said he told her that, when he had a sale, he increased the price of some of the things. His daughter worked in Jolly's in Bath.

Wilfred Hartley, born 1922

The Beales at Hyde

The Beale family came from Newent to live at Hyde Court around 200 years ago. It was one large house then, but it's been divided up since.

I was born just after my great aunt, Dorothea Beale, died. She was a pioneer of education, and was headmistress of Cheltenham Ladies College. I always found it amusing that, in those days, anyone could go to the Ladies College if their father was in trade, but *not* if they had their name above the shop.

I was born in Wimbledon, but my father moved the family to Minchinhampton in 1921 when I was fourteen. We lived in The Yews, which is now Blueboys. There were four of us children – two boys and two girls, and we were thrilled at the thought of living in the country. We already knew Minchinhampton fairly well as we'd often stayed with grandfather at Hyde Court. He kept a couple of horses, pigs and a cow, and I can remember making butter there – you made all your own butter. There was a gardener because they grew all their own fruit and veg. We loved staying at Hyde Court, and the highlight for us children was always going to tea with the maids. They had a huge and beautiful kitchen, which you reached through a green baize door. We had great fun with them.

My grandfather was stone deaf from the time he was five, after contracting scarlet fever. He went over to Canada where he married his wife who was also stone deaf. The then-owner of Hyde Court was Miss Eliza Beale, his sister, who told my grandfather that, if he came with his family to live with her, she would leave him the house. My grandfather had six children, and he was worried about what would happen to them and to his wife if he were to die, so they all moved to Hyde Court in about 1900.

I remember being told a story about him. He was walking from Hyde to Bussage and, in those days, you would go over the road, over the canal and over the railway before you could walk up the other side. This one day, he was walking down when he saw a man he knew, on the other side of the line, throw up his arms to stop him going further.

Hyde Court.

Gladys Beale on the mounting block – which is still to be seen at Hyde Court – with her uncle, Maurice Hayward, who was killed in the First World War, in 1916.

He stopped, only to see a train rushing past him. Luckily this man had known my grandfather was deaf, because if he had shouted grandfather wouldn't have heard and he'd have been killed.

We used to get a train from Stroud to Paddington, which cost 10s for a day return. We travelled in great comfort – you could have your breakfast on the train – and they were never late.

When we first came down, we had bicycles, of course, and a pony and trap. In those days, your friends were all at the end of a bike ride – we knew very few people on the other side of the hill. Nobody had a car except for Dr Brown.

Dr Brown moved here just before the First World War with the idea that it would be a light job, but it never was. There were no telephones, so he would drive over to see a patient in Bisley, come back to Minchinhampton, only to be called out again to Bisley. He used to find it so tiresome, because he was backwards and forwards in his car all the time. The Browns lived in Well Hill and had the surgery there. They used to make up all their own medicines.

My father got his first car in 1923. It's extraordinary, the things that you remember, but it was a Humber with the number plate PF2023. It was such a thrill, and I think people were quite envious because there weren't many with a car. Mr Walker had a cycle shop where the Coffee Bean now is, and he had a taxi. And Mr Merritt, who had a garage at the top of Windmill Road, drove a bus on a Saturday morning. My sister and I went from here to Stroud on it to go to have dancing lessons. We all used to have to sit sideways, facing each other.

Those were the great days of ballroom dancing, and we used to go from house to

The Beale family: Gladys stands with her mother, Leila, and her father, Miles, who is on the far right of the photograph.

house to attend dances. The Richardsons had one at Beaudesert, and the Duguids at Box House. Everyone had their own tennis courts – we had one, the Browns had one and so did the Rectory. You'd ask about ten people round and we used to play tennis quite seriously. My father was a very good tennis player, and he played at Wimbledon when it was a club.

The village school was very good but basic, so I was sent to boarding school. My sister and four little girls had a governess, and my brothers went to Oakley Hall. We always had a cook and a maid, but I remember my mother used to get in extra help in the holidays. My brothers were very keen on cricket, and they used to cycle to Cirencester, carrying their bats on their

bikes. Once they had a nasty accident when they ran into each other, which was very tiresome for both bats and boys!

Gladys Beale, born 1907

The Gunpowder Plot

There's a story that's still told around the pubs in Nailsworth to this day. I know it to be true, because it happened when I was a little boy.

There was a fellow living at Harley Wood who discovered that someone was pinching his wood from outside his house. Of course, everybody used logs of wood in those days. Well, he watched for a couple of nights, but he couldn't catch anyone. So he thought of a plan. He drilled a couple of holes in several blocks of wood, and filled them with gunpowder. Somebody took them – and it blew their grate out. So they couldn't really argue about that, could they?

Herby Creed, born 1917

Frying Tonight

There were lots of shops I remember in Nailsworth. Harts ladies' shop was exclusive and expensive. Then there was Daunceys men's shop, and Yarnolds, which catered more for the working bloke. Freshwaters was the grocer's shop by Market Street. Frankie Smith ran that, and he used to take the local club money. If you were ill, or if you badly needed money, you could borrow against that.

Harold Fletcher had a fish shop where William's Kitchen is now. Any fish he didn't sell, he would fry it up in the fryer at the back, and you could get fish and chips for tuppence, wrapped in newspaper. He was a big bloke, smart-looking, who used to live up Forest Green. He had no freezers or fridges. The fish used to lie on a steel tray with fresh water running over it from a pipe, with a gutter at the bottom. The water used to run down the street. We weren't as hygienic then, but I remember one thing: the drains used to be cleaned out every week, unlike now.

We used to get buskers who'd go round singing in the street. Some would play concertinas, and they used to collect money. They were rough, but you were never afraid of them. That all stopped after the war.

'Gypoons' used to come round selling pegs and things. They were all right. Most of

An original paper bag for wrapping purchases from Shipway, the ladies' outfitters.

them had black hair and dark skins, but you never saw one wearing glasses. The wood smoke from the fires they used to cook on made their eyes good. They lived in those tiny caravans dragged by horses.

Norman Vick, born 1914

The Inconveniences

Mum was called Muriel Leonard, and she came from a big family with at least six girls and two boys. All the girls slept in one bedroom with three double beds. They lived at Egypt Mill, in the old manor house that had been divided up. Before she married, mum worked as a silver-mounter at Walkers Sticks in Dunkirk Mill.

When we were children, we went up to see her parents – Fred and Jessie Leonard – every Sunday. We'd try and avoid using their toilets. They were in a hut used by all the people who lived there, and they were straight over the water. There were two sizes of opening, one for a child and one for an adult. You can imagine what it must have been like in the Nailsworth flood. The water came up to the keyboard of their piano. We went the day after, and I saw the mark round the wall. The only redeeming feature was that the floors were flagstones.

Wilfred Hartley, born 1922

Down to the End of the Garden

We had no bathroom. At Tetbury Street, there was an outside loo right at the top of the garden. It was just a hole in the ground. We made a wooden frame to sit on, and then you just threw water down. The hole went right down through a hole in the rocks. The people two houses down from here had buckets that they had to empty in the garden. In the winter, we used to have a candle in a jam jar. You'd get halfway up the garden, and the candle would go out!

When I was courting, Norman's family had a big garden that ended in a wood. To go to the toilet at the end of the garden, I used to take the dog. It was awful – I was frightened to death. There were lots of tramps around, and I was always scared I'd find a tramp in there.

May Vick (née Beard), born 1918

Using the Potty

We had to go and visit a certain family who lived locally on a farm, but they didn't have plumbing there. On one occasion, my eldest sister had to use the loo. They didn't have one, and she was told she'd have to use a potty. She made a frightful scene and refused. The poor wife of the farmer was highly embarrassed.

Lady Mary Rawlinson (née Hill), born 1923

Being Frugal

My great grandmother was a very hard woman, probably because they didn't have very much. She was a weaver at Longfords for many years. She was Francis Furley's wife, the shoemaker. He would walk around the area and measure up feet.

They had quite a large garden where they grew fruit and veg. When they had surplus, they used to make an earth clamp. You dug out an area and lined it with straw, and put in potatoes and carrots, then you covered them with straw and earth. That would seal it and preserve it. When they had a lot of fruit, they would sell it. My mother said that, every Saturday night, her grandmother would empty her purse, and every farthing would go into a box. Then she would take her housekeeping out of Francis's income from shoes. They finished up owning five houses in Box and one in Nailsworth, and it was only done by being frugal. They were Baptists at Minchinhampton, and Francis helped to build the chapel there. They gave both time and money to it.

My mother said her grandmother once gave her a basket of windfalls, which were no bigger than golf balls, as any that were larger were sold for a few coppers. My mother remembered going home and slamming them down on the table, saying, 'Our granny sent these out of the sheer generosity of her heart!'

Vera Harvey (née Smith), born 1934

Cutting a Dash

I remember the first motorcar in Box. It belonged to Mr Fyffe at Trulwell House and he employed a chauffeur named Bob Whitehead. But cars were not so powerful in those days, so that when they got to the steepest part of the Halfway House hill, the

Helping to build the Institute in Minchinhampton: the Furley brothers are the two bearded gentleman on the far right of the seated row.

The famous fruit importer, Mr Fyffe, and his family at home in Box.

passengers had to get out and walk, while the chauffeur drove up to the top and waited for them to walk up. But Mr Fyffe soon altered this arrangement by cutting a roadway out of the back of his premises and across the Common, coming out near Hampton Green. This way, needless to say, was not so steep.

Harold Heiron, born 1902

A Bath Made for Two

One of my jobs was inspecting housing. There was one family with about seven children, where the husband was nearly always unemployed. The wife did bits and pieces. A lot of the time the children had bare feet. It was a private house – we had to treat the place for fleas.

Another family, who were in a council house in Forest Green, applied for a larger property. I arranged to meet them to show them a house in Park Road. His wife was very interested, but he said, 'It's no bloody good. The bath's not big enough for the two of us to get in together'. So he wouldn't take it. I had to keep a straight face, of course.

Alan Denman, born 1921

Nailsworth Mystery Shopping Man

My mother shopped at Freshwater and at Prices, which were family businesses in Market Street. Our favourite shop was where Watermans Restaurant is – Miss Witchell's sweet shop. She was known as Aunty Dot, and that's where we went to spend our Saturday penny. She was a round person, very calm and kind, and she also sold a small selection of toys. That's where we bought our spinning tops. Aunty Dot had a room at the back of her shop where she had a parrot in a cage. We were allowed to go in and see it occasionally. There was a toyshop where the clock tower now stands. It had a canopy running all along the front. It was part of the wool shop run by Miss Smith.

There was another blacksmith's behind what is now the cycle shop on The Cross, and the pig sties were behind there too. The animals were kept there before they went to slaughter.

Each year there was a Nailsworth Shopping Week close to Christmas. I think the shops would have competitions in the windows. We were allowed to go out in the dark, which was very exciting, to find the Mystery Man. He would go round the streets, and, if you thought you'd found him, you had to go up and address him with certain words: 'You are the Nailsworth Mystery Shopping Man'. If you were right, you won some money.

When we had really hot summers, a horse and cart used to come round, with a water tank on the top, and water would be sprayed on the streets to keep the dust down. The man who drove it was Mr Sysum, and I can still remember the smell – quite a nice smell – of it laying the dust.

Dorothy Blair (née Bruton), born 1921

Send Them a Week's Notice

In Minchinhampton Market Square, there used to be a big weighing concern and a little hut where the loads would come in – swedes, turnips, hay – and John King from Nailsworth used to come through and stop there and the weight be checked. From there, in latter days, was what we used to call The Islands, which has been pulled down and the Monument put in its place.

A view of the old wool shop, run by Miss Smith.

Thompsons used to run a clothier's. Just above the clothier's shop there used to be a stables where the boys, when they did come to a certain age, used to have a little bit of a club. Minchinhampton used to have billiards there. There was Ernie Newman's father – he was in charge, the caretaker there. Then they had a rifle range there. They used to go in these competitions, like the league.

Then there was Reed – he was getting on in years. On a Sunday morning, Clarkes from the White Horse used to come down and go to chapel and thoroughly enjoy the service there and, on a dinnertime, Reed had the horse and the trap there, all ready to take them home.

Another thing I would like to point out to you, there was the old fire brigade under Captain Webb that lived in The Buildings – that was Park Terrace. One day, there was a message came through that there was a fire going, and they had to send down to Captain Webb to know where the keys was belonging to the fire gates before they could be opened. Well the fire was still burning, and you can take it from me now, I think the best thing that they could have done in years gone by was, if you were going to have a fire, then send them a week's notice.

George Ellins, born 1897

A Burning Issue

I can remember going into Nailsworth to Fryers the grocery shop, by the kettle, and I would have an order from my grandmother. Mr Birt, who used to live at the top of Whips Lane, used to bring up the groceries on his way home.

My grandfather used to go down to Fryers,

Pipe-smoking George Woodward, pictured in 1947 with his grandson Ron, Margery's cousin, who is also a contributor to this book.

which was the sort of shop where he could get out his pocketknife and try the cheeses. One day, he went in and said, 'I can smell something burning in here!' They pointed out to him he had his pipe in his waistcoat pocket that was still burning. He smoked a pipe until he died.

There was a sweet shop up on The Cross. And we used to go to the Co-op at the bottom of Bath Road with my mother to get groceries. With a bit of luck, we would get two pennyworth of Granny's Dumps which were three-cornered sweets – yellow with brown stripes. They were minty things.

Margery Woodward, born 1929

The Revd Sammy Ford and his wife.

Remembering the Poet's Wife

My mother bought our house, Glendower, from Mrs Helen Mathilda Davies, my great aunt by marriage, in the 1940s. The house is 300 to 400 years old. It started as a one-up, one-down, and even now it's not changed much since Mrs Davies lived there. There's still an old built-in dresser in the kitchen.

My great uncle, the poet W.H. Davies, married Helen in 1923 when he was about fifty-three – some thirty years older than his wife. I think she first met him at a bus stop. She might have married him partly because he was famous.

She went to live in Harrogate in the 1940s, then moved to Bournemouth. She used to come back to visit Nailsworth for quite a long time, but she didn't always stay with us. Sometimes she stayed at the George, and sometimes at The Shears in Watledge. I remember a man called Mr Parker who was the publican there.

Mrs Davies was very short and fairly fat, and she used to repeat the same stories. She didn't seem to speak naturally – perhaps she was trying to be grand. I suppose she might have thought herself a lady of importance. I don't really remember my great uncle. He died when I was about seven.

Norman Phillips, born 1933

Public Baths

We left Parson's Court when I was five, and moved to the Institute next to Minchinhampton Baptist Church. My father took over the caretakership, so we lived rent-free. The Institute was built in 1907 for young men, to get them out of the pubs. There was a billiards table, and there were draughts and darts and table tennis. In the Institute there were three public baths and a huge geyser in the wall and a massive tank of water. People could come in and have a bath for sixpence. Each bath was in a cubicle, and there were lashings of hot water. It was well used at the weekends.

The Revd E.F. Forsdike was the minister. He had two sons and a daughter. One son was a pilot in the war. A previous minister, the Revd Sammy Ford, went to prison in protest against paying part of his taxes. I think it was the tax on drainage that he didn't agree with. Anyway, he went to jail, but was bailed out by one of his congregation – probably against his wishes.

We had an outside 'lav', but it was a flush one – quite a luxury in those days. It was dodgy when we had snow. There were tiled roofs in the Institute, and the snow would hang over the edge, so you had to run the gauntlet to get to the toilet before it slid off.

Iris Dyer (née Ellins), born 1930

Not in My House

I can remember reading about the Mitfords – they were always in the papers. All the exciting bits were in the *News of the World* but my father wouldn't allow that paper in the house.

Gladys Beale, born 1907

Uninvited Guests

My parents, Thomas and Kate Gardiner, were the first caretakers of the Institute, moving in during the summer of 1907 with my two sisters – Nellie, who was six years old, and Evelyn, just six weeks old. Our brother, Reg, was born in June 1909, and I arrived just before Christmas 1912.

We were a happy, close-knit family, and our parents brought us up in the 'nurture and admonition of the Lord' as they had pledged to do.

Life was not without its hazards! There were no cattle grids in those days to keep animals confined to The Park, so when the weather was hot, it was a common sight to see horses and cows wandering round the streets, seeking whatever shade they could find. A young heifer found its way around the house one day when I was about six months old, and tipped up the bassinet in which I was sleeping. Fortunately – so I was told – I landed on pillows and came to no harm.

A partially-glazed door in the living room opened on to a yard at the back of the house, and during a heat wave the doors were wide open, including the front door. Several times a cow or a horse wandered round the house and, finding no room to retreat, would pass through the open door, through the living room, through the passage, and out through the front door to the street. Fortunately, cars were few and far between in those early days after the Great War.

The downstairs rooms were lit with old-fashioned gas mantles, but we had candles to 'light us to bed'. No central heating, of course; coal fires downstairs, and an oil heater to take the chill off the air in the bedrooms during the winter months.

The Revd Sammy Ford, doing his bit during the building of the Institute.

The volunteer workers who helped to build the Institute in 1907.

The Baptist Chapel congregation, with building work for the Institute clearly on-going in the background.

I have vivid memories of my brother being ill with scarlet fever and confined to his bedroom on the top floor of the house for six weeks. Mum refused to allow him to go to the isolation hospital, preferring to nurse him herself, although it meant climbing two flights of stairs innumerable times a day. He was strictly 'out of bounds' for the rest of us, but curiosity got the better of me, and I crept up the stairs one day, and was horrified to be met with a white sheet smelling of strong disinfectant, completely covering the bedroom door.

The children who lived next door were our playmates, and we frequently got into scrapes. It was always through disobedience – what a painful lesson to learn! There was a large wooden mangle in the shed which we were forbidden to touch, but it was fun to turn the handle and feed things through the wooden rollers, until one day the inevitable happened, and the girl from next door got one of her fingers trapped in the cogs. Needless to say, we were sent to bed in disgrace. On another occasion, I decided to chop some firewood, and nearly lost the top of my thumb. I think mum was so overcome at the sight of blood, that I didn't get the ticking off I so richly deserved.

Winifred Glassonbury (née Gardiner), born 1912

Seeing the Light

In 1937, a man came round asking if we wanted electricity. He said they couldn't bring it up unless everyone had it. You had to pay a sum to be installed, which you could do at once, or in instalments which cost a bit extra.

You had to have a light put in each room – that was one of the conditions they laid on. But my stepmother wouldn't let us have a bulb in the children's bedroom. And woe betide us if we turned the switch on because all the electricity would come out. We couldn't convince her that, if there was no bulb, the electricity wouldn't be used. She thought it worked just like gas!

Stan Dyer, born 1925

If You Want to Get Ahead, Get a Duck

There's a lovely story that was told to me about a man who said to his wife not to get anything for the weekend as he was going to kill one of his ducks. She said that was fine, and off he went down to where he kept the ducks, on a pond on the edge of Harley Wood.

His axe was down there, because he used it for chopping wood, so he decided to use that to kill the duck, rather than to wring its neck. He got the duck's head on a chopping block, but they're pretty strong, hefty birds, so he put his knee on its back – though not firmly enough. He brought the axe down and did the job very neatly. But when he looked, all he had left was the head. The duck's nervous system that works when they're killed had meant the duck had taken off. They found the body lodged in one of the branches of a tree, but too high for them to reach it!

Vera Harvey (nee Smith), born 1934

CHAPTER 3

Difficult Days

Stan Dyer (on far left of picture), with his father and stepmother, brothers and sisters.

Ask No Questions

When I was six years old, we were got out of bed early in the morning. My sister was in charge – she was sixteen – and she said, 'I've got to take you off to Aunty Phyllis's' – me and the next boy up.

I said, 'What have we got to go for?' and she said, 'Don't ask questions and you'll be told no lies' which was what we were always told in those days. Off we went up to Aunty Phyllis's at France Lynch with a change of clothes. We hadn't a clue why or how long we were going for.

She had a fairly big family as well – five children – and she didn't really have room. When we went to bed at night, my brother and myself got into one bed and, between us, was cousin Valerie. We didn't think much of that, but she thought it was great.

We were taken to Chalford Hill School, and I think we must have been there two months. Aunty Phyllis was nice, but we wanted to go home. There were good bits. We never had pocket money at home, but Aunty Phyllis's eldest son, Jack, was at work, and he used to give us all a penny on Monday, and a ha'penny on Wednesdays, which was enough for a bar of chocolate.

Then came the day when we were told we were going home. I went bouncing into the house and looked all the way round. 'Where's our mum?' My sister said, 'She's gone to be with Jesus'.

I was stunned. I didn't ask questions. I was speechless. I never even cried. My sister took over, and was taken away from work. She used to look after dad and the rest of us. Looking back, I must have been very unhappy. That year is almost a blank in my mind.

A year after that, we were sent to Minchinhampton, to Aunty Flo. We were told we had to be there all day, but we didn't know why. She was a nice lady who lived in Friday Street. Just as we were going home, Aunty Flo said, 'When you get home, you'll meet your new mother'. We'd seen her before, because we had visited her two or three times at her home in Cheltenham, but we'd no idea she was going to be our mum.

All was well for a while, but it wasn't ideal. She was a spinster and she'd had a nice home, but she'd come into a terrible environment. She couldn't cope, and I don't blame her, and it made her harsh.

There wasn't any love there. Dad was becoming remote. He had to provide for us, but he didn't have to provide any love – he just couldn't, I suppose. They didn't seem to think we children had any feelings.

We went through this ritual once again about a year later – going up to Aunty Phyllis's for a few weeks. We knew our stepmother hadn't died, because she got us ready to go. When we came back, there was a baby in the house – a new little baby sister. We'd had no idea our stepmother was going to have a baby. They weren't cruel parents – they were just not loving. Our father never hit us once. He just brought us up the way he'd been brought up.

Stan Dyer, born 1925

'There's Been an Accident'

My brothers and sisters were all coming home from Sunday School, when mother heard someone scream. She had no idea what it was, but she said to my dad, 'There's been an accident, Joe, go and see what's happened'. Dad went running across the field, only to find that it was his own daughter, Mary. He took her up to Dr Brown's surgery in Minchinhampton, which was in what is now Dr Brown's Road, and then she was transferred to Stroud Hospital.

Mum would often talk about Mary, saying what a pretty little girl she was. She was only five when she died, which was the year before I was born. My mother kept all the letters of condolence that she received, and I've still got them now.

Sheila Jarman (née Smith), born 1931

Infants' School.
Minchinhampton.
June 23rd 1930

Dear Mrs Smith,

I am extremely sorry to hear of your very great trouble. The news was a terrible shock to me this morning. Words fail to express how grieved and sorry both the teachers and children are about the accident which happened to little Mary. We shall miss her very much, she was such a happy contented little girl but we shall think of her now as safe with Jesus in a happier home.

Our deepest sympathy is for you and your family in your great sorrow.

An eminently touching letter from Miss Jukes, Mary's teacher at Minchinhampton School.

High St
Minchinhampton
June 23

Dear Mr and Mrs Smith,

My wife and son wish to join with me in sending our very kindest sympathy with you in the sad time you are having through the death of your dear little Mary. When I used to go my walks, on Sunday afternoons, I always met them going to Sunday School, and we usually had a little chat. Mary was a little toddler then but I looked upon them as my young friends. I pray the Lord Jesus will comfort you in your sad trials and lead you to feel she is gone to Him. To Him who said Let the little children come unto me for of such is the Kingdom of Heaven. With kindest regards and sympathy from us all.

Yours sincerely,
F.C. Hughes

The Gables
Minchinhampton
Glos
June 25

Dear Mrs Smith,

I must write a line to tell you how deeply I sympathise with you and your husband in the tragic death of your dear little girl. I

Mary Smith in a photograph taken shortly before she was so tragically killed.

have lost 2 children myself, and I know too well all the sorrow and suffering it means for you all. You have been such a good mother in bringing your children so regularly to the Infant Welfare, that we all know your little ones and what a happy family you are and it makes one realize all the more what this sorrow means to you.

It must be a comfort to you to feel that your little girl did not suffer, and that she is safe and happy now.

With much sympathy,

Yours sincerely
Hylda Elton

Greylands
Minchinhampton
Stroud, Glos.
24 June 1930

Dear Mrs Smith,

I cannot tell you how terribly distressed we all are for you and Mr Smith in this awful blow.

I only heard of it last night and it has haunted me ever since. One can only hope that your dear little girl did not suffer consciously – it is heart-rending to think of that tiny mite of five years old trying to save those younger than herself. I was watching her at Gatcombe and thought then what a sweet little face she had – she was so intent in watching the other children. She must have been such a dear little mother to her brothers and sisters.

I cannot express myself: you will understand – our deepest sympathy is with you. I will come and see you on Saturday if I may. I don't like to come now but I did want

ROAD FATALITY.

INQUEST ON CHILD VICTIM.

JURY AND RIDER'S "INSUFFICIENT CARE."

Sitting with a jury at Stroud Petty Sessional Court this morning, the Divisional Coroner (Mr. J. R. Morton Ball) conducted an inquiry into the circumstances of the death of Emily Mary Smith (5), daughter of Mr. Joseph Smith, of Woeful Dane Farm, Minchinhampton, who was the victim of the motor-cycling fatality on the Tetbury-road when returning home with other scholars from Sunday School on Sunday afternoon.

The jury returned a verdict of accidental death, but added that they considered that insufficient care was exercised by the rider of the motor-cycle, Roger Wilfred Mustoe, of Babdown Cottages, Beverstone, near Tetbury, having regard to the number of children about at the time. Mustoe was censured by the Coroner.

Father's Evidence.

One of the press cuttings from a local paper, kept by Mary Smith's grieving mother, Maud.

you to know that we are so horrified – you have been always such a good appreciative member of the welfare and on its behalf and on my own, do I send these few poor words. We sorrow with you.

Yours truly,
Muriel R. Trollope

Pte Norman Vick, with the 10th Battalion, Glosters, taken during the Second World War.

When Mary Smith was Killed

I remember when Mary Smith was killed. We were all at Sunday School together. There were several of them walking in a group – because Mary was with her sister and her brothers – going round Woefuldane corner. It was a rare event, especially as she was killed by a motorbike – there weren't many of them around then.

It was very sad at the chapel. All the children went to the funeral. I can see them now. All the Smith girls had little black and white dresses and white Panama hats. They weren't so wealthy that they could buy things easily – probably their mother made them.

It was a shattering time. They were a close family – a very big family. They lived at the farm, played at the farm and stayed on the farm.

May Vick (née Beard), born 1918

When Gladys Died

There used to be fireplaces in school, and they would riddle the ashes in the playground. A cousin of mine, Gladys Clark, fell over in the playground. She died, and I think it was from blood poisoning – I'm sure it was those ashes. I went to see her in her coffin, which was open in her home. I was about nine at the time, and I went because we played together. It wasn't a frightening experience – we didn't look upon death like you do.

Muriel Newman (née Davis), born 1916

On the Labour

I left school at fourteen in Christmas 1928, and I took up until Easter to get a job. There was a slump on, and everyone was out of work. I used to go rabbiting and sell rabbits round the village. You would make traps with a wire noose and put them in the woods and fields. Little rabbits cost sixpence, and the big ones ninepence. If they had the skin, it was an extra tuppence. People would make fur gloves with that.

We used to go 'stowling' too. In the big woods, they would cut trees down and leave a stump. After twelve months, it would dry and you could cut it up with an axe. You

William Heiron who 'had no mother', sitting cross-legged, surrounded by lads from Nailsworth in the 1870s.

would use them like logs, and we used to sell them a shilling a bag.

Then I got a job at the pin mill at Frogmarsh, Woodchester. We had to look after the machines to make sure they kept going. I wore short trousers when I started work because they were cheaper than long trousers.

At the pin mill, you worked one week, then had a week on the Labour because they were short of work. After twelve months I was out of work again, and that meant going down to the Labour. The manager there was an old devil. He was an ex-Naval officer, and he used to say to the men, 'You haven't been looking for work!' More than one man would have liked to have grabbed him round the neck, but they didn't dare. He treated them like dirt.

The factories would send to the Labour if they wanted anyone. If you didn't take the job, they stopped your Labour pay.

Norman Vick, born 1914

Abandoned by a Charlatan

My grandfather, William Heiron, who was from Box, was born in the July, his parents were married in the August, and his father died aged twenty-one in the November – of exhaustion and debility. His mother, Emily, was a charlatan. She tried to get every penny. When her husband died, she told the person laying him out that there was a sheet in the top drawer of the chest of drawers.

The person opened the wrong drawer, and found it was full of sovereigns.

Emily went to Lawyer Smith – the one the Nailsworth fountain is dedicated to – because he was in charge of the estate. She told him 'I need more money to bring up little William', and he gave her an allowance. She went back and told him she couldn't manage, so Lawyer Smith told her to go to the outfitters in Nailsworth and to send him the bill. That was stopped when the lawyer found out she was selling the clothes. When William was three or four years old, she took him to her parents and asked them to look after him for a while. No-one ever saw her again.

He lived with his grandparents until they died, and by then he was nine. And so the lawyer paid various people in the village for him to live in their homes until he was out of his apprenticeship.

When he was thirteen, my grandfather was apprenticed to a carpenter in Amberley. He did a lot of work in Amberley Church. He used to have to go out mid-morning to get beer from the nearest pub for the carpenter, for his morning and his lunchtime drink.

When William married my grandmother and he'd built their house – the one I still live in – he told her he was going to take four or six months out and get work in Manchester because that's where people thought his mother had gone. He searched for her, but he couldn't find her, so he said he hadn't got a mother.

Years later, he got some letters from Manchester. They said that his mother had died and what a wonderful person she had been. And they all asked him to send money for the funeral.

Vera Harvey (née Smith), born 1934

Fighting the Flood

I remember the flood of 1931. I was out in all of it. I was fourteen, and I'd been to Nailsworth show as usual. There was a thunderstorm, and it was bucketing down. I got through it to the 'Brit', and I was up to my thighs in water. It was very frightening, because the water was flowing so fast. It was pouring down from Newmarket, and down the Avening and Horsley valleys. It lifted the manhole covers up.

You could see tins of biscuits and packets of butter floating past. My Aunt Mary had a grocery shop on the Horsley Road that was down some steps at a very low point. There was a brook at the bottom of her garden and fisheries nearby, and she was washed out.

I had a job selling newspapers at the time. Father had got the concession for them – the *Gloucester Journal* and the *Stroud Journal*. I remember thinking how funny it was, because hundreds of people came down to see the flood, and yet they still wanted to buy the newspapers to see the pictures afterwards. So I did a roaring trade for a couple of weeks.

The flood happened late in the day, so it was the next morning when people could see what had happened. It was a filthy sight. Most people in the Brit Square were there clearing out rubbish.

Herby Creed, born 1917

We Lost our Shoes

We didn't have any shoes left in the flood. The stream ran underneath our house in Cossack Square, and, during the flood, a trap door in the house blew open and took

Cossack Square, Nailsworth, which Herby Creed remembers being flooded in 1931.

away all the shoes in the shoe cupboard. The water came right through the house, and the smell the next morning was pretty horrific. It went into the ironmonger's shop, too, and it took ages to get rid of the smell. There was a huge hole in front of the Brit. We found it very exciting. We were all shipped up to an aunt in the Bristol Road while they cleaned up.

Dorothy Blair (née Bruton), born 1921

The Flood of 1931

I can remember the flood of 1931. My mum took my brother and me to the horse show. It rained and rained. There was a girl called Nellie Porter who used to live next door to us, who'd got married and had rooms next to Hilliers shop. She said we could come in her flat until it eased off. It was torrential, with thunder and lightning.

I was about fourteen, and my mum said I had better sleep in my brother's bed because it was so frightening. I could hear the stones going down the back of the house.

I was going on an outing the next day, and, as we went, we saw gullies where our friend's path had been washed away. There used to be a Mr Workman going on the buses, and we saw him walking with his canary in a cage. He had to take it with him because his home was flooded out.

Muriel Newman (née Davis), born 1916

The Stigma of TB

When I was at school, TB was about. Two people who attended Minchinhampton School died from it while still in their 'teens. People who had the disease used to live in chalets in their gardens with their doors wide open – they never shut them because you were supposed to have lots of fresh air. One girl who lived in Box Lane was in a chalet for several years. It looked like a wooden shed with windows like in a cricket pavilion.

I don't know of anyone who had TB who survived. My father had it. He was at home for a long while, but his nerves started to go, and his doctor sent him to the sanatorium. That was a chalet block, with the doors open in all weathers. While my father was there, they brought in a fellow he'd been at school with. He said to my father, 'I feel as if I've had a night in the cow shed!'

People who had the disease were shunned, and I remember when I started courting, Tom's father had drilled into him that he wasn't to go near any family who'd had TB – he wasn't to get involved. His father told him, 'Don't be rude, be polite – but keep away'. When he told his father that mine had died of TB, a look came over his father's face and he said, 'Look, if you think anything of the girl, don't drop her for that'. It was the turning point for him.

When the lungs were in danger, there was a treatment where they would fill them with some substance mixed in with gold dust. My parents considered this –

GREAT STORM DISASTER

THOUSANDS OF POUNDS DAMAGE AT NAILSWORTH

FLOODS AND WRECKAGE IN MAIN STREETS

CLOUD BURST CAUSES SERIOUS FLOODS

A TERRIFIC thunderstorm, the worst experienced for many years, broke over Glo'stershire on Tuesday, causing widespread damage and considerable inconvenience to traffic.

The storm passing over Nailsworth wrought indescribable destruction and caused thousands of pounds damage to property. A cloud burst, streams overflowed their banks, drains were unable to cope with the deluge, and the streets soon resembled rivers, shops and other property being flooded to a depth of several feet of water.

The headline of one of many newspaper stories that catalogued the disastrous flood of 1931.

they would have had to have paid – but it was really all too late for my father.

Before my time, in my grandmother's time, there was a man called Black Jacob. He used to go into the woods and collect big slugs. He would slime them, and use the slime to make a medicine you drank. That was supposed to be a cure for TB. He was a herbalist, and people would buy his potions for a ha'penny a time.

My mother's great grandfather on her mother's side was the last of the cottage weavers. His son, Francis Furley, was a shoemaker and he served for many years on the parish council. There was a case of smallpox in the village – a son of a Box couple had come home from sea and, of course, he had to be in isolation for that. My great grandfather had to go down to their house where the woman would put a basket on the wall with a shopping list and money, all wrapped in a vinegar cloth. My great-grandfather would do their shopping for them and put the basket back on the wall. He was given two ounces of tobacco a week by the parish council for doing that, and he was told he had to be smoking when he went near the house as a protection against smallpox.

Vera Harvey (née Smith), born 1934

In the Fever Hospital

When I was fifteen, I was in the fever hospital at Cashes Green for ten weeks because they thought I was a carrier of diphtheria. I'd had trouble with my ears which wouldn't heal, and they took swabs, and that was what the swabs revealed.

I wasn't in bed, but it was very

A happy, healthy, May Vick whose long life has defied her one-time spell in the 'fever hospital'.

Archie Kirby, in 1959 (second from right) with his brothers and sisters.

restricted. We had a matron we were all frightened to death of. The wards were kept spotless – all polished and clean by ten o'clock in the morning. There were open fires with grates that had to be polished and lit.

The food was very good, and hospital was where I learned to eat cabbage. I couldn't stand any green stuff when I was little, but you ate everything up there!

There were four of us who were meant to be carriers, and we were in a ward with grown-ups and children with diphtheria. Further up was a big open block and that was where they brought bad cases of TB. They used to say that if you were taken up to Cashes Green, then there was no cure. They more or less slept in the fresh air.

Then there was another ward for scarlet fever, which we didn't dare go near.

It was January time when I was there, and no visitors could come into the ward. They had to stand on a step outside the window, shivering, and talk to you through that. If they had brought you anything, they had to hand it in at the door.

May Vick (née Beard), born 1918

Off To War

When the First World War broke out, they had recruitment sessions in all the villages. Colonel Ricardo organized one, and he stood on a platform in the Market Square asking for volunteers. My brother got up and volunteered, but my father stood up and said, 'You can't have him! He's only seventeen'. But Archie went into Stroud the next day and joined up.

Whenever he came home on leave, we were told not to ask him when he was going back. He'd come home in the middle of the night, after walking up from Stroud station. I can still remember how upset my mother was every time he had to go back. But he went right through the war without being injured.

Jessie Kirby, born 1909

A Cow's Blood Transfusion

My grandmother's cousin, Alf Latham, was a plasterer and tiler, and he took work in Australia in about 1905. He had this fall where he came off his ladder and landed on his head, fracturing his skull. Medicine in Australia was very primitive, but they operated and put a plate in his head. He needed a blood transfusion, and they were very few and far between. So they gave him cows' blood. His father had to pay for a doctor to travel with him by sea, and bring him back home.

The damage to the brain left him with depression and epileptic fits. Every time he had these fits, my mother said, he would go round and round in circles, and he would low like a cow. He was about twenty or thirty when this happened, and he lived into his seventies. Within a few years of the accident, he could hold a job down, and Fred Stevens gave him a job in his yard.

Vera Harvey (née Smith), born 1934

Taken Away From School

I went to Horsley School until I was nine, and then I won a scholarship to Stroud Central School. My parents were so pleased – but I was the only one without a uniform. I got teased terribly for that. And I had cut-down boots. Boots in those days were long lace-up ones that had little clips on to do them up. I was walking along the canal once, when one of the boys called out, 'You've got girls' boots on'. Men's boots had a little tag on the back to pull them on, and mine didn't.

To get to school, I walked from Wallow Green to the railway, and then I'd catch the Dudbridge Donkey. I'd get off at Dudbridge and then I'd walk further than I rode to get to school.

I was taken away from Central School after two or three years because father wanted someone to take the papers round and get some more money for the family. I went back to Horsley School so that, every evening, I could pick up the papers at Nailsworth when the van came in. I delivered them round Nailsworth, Horsley, Shortwood, Rockness and Washpool after school each day on a bike. It took me two hours.

Herby Creed, born 1917

The Worst School Bullies

I went to Brimscombe School, which was a harsh place. I was bullied, but by the teachers not by the pupils. I used to walk home by myself, even at four, down Water Lane, through the trees and up through the field. It was getting on for a mile, but it was no bother at all. I never felt threatened.

A young Stan Dyer, during his days at Brimscombe School.

The head had a cane, which he enjoyed using for quite trivial things. The classes were divided by glass partitions and, one day, there was a bit of an uproar in the next class. Everyone was laughing about something. I stood up to look, and the head came through the door. He said, 'Come out here, Dyer!' I knew what was going to happen next. He held your fingers steady, and the cane came down hard. You normally had one stroke on each hand, and in the playground you would boast that it didn't hurt – 'It would take more than that to hurt me' – I was, of course, lying. It hurt so much you had difficulty in holding your pen.

The trouble was, the head had whipping boys, and it was generally speaking the poorer boys who caught it. You'd know that so-and-so was a little blighter, but he'd get away with it, probably because his father went to church with the headmaster.

When I was about six or seven, my teacher spotted that I was left-handed, and she set about 'curing' me. You can understand how difficult it was trying to keep up with your right hand when you're left-handed, so I'd quickly switch hands back to catch up. Down would come the ruler, smack on my fingers. I didn't want to defy her; I just couldn't do it. It got to the point where I was afraid to go to school.

One day, the head came in and saw her smacking me with a ruler. She said to him, 'I can't get him to write with his right hand'. He said, 'If he's naturally left-handed, leave him alone'. And that was the end of that.

I was slightly bow-legged, and when we went out to drill, I was ordered to put my knees together. Well, I couldn't do that, either.

On the bright side, Miss Webb came. She was a lovely teacher. I'd go out of my way to walk to school with her and carry her case. You can work hard for someone you like. She was kind and, if you got stuck, she would sit down and show you.

We used to do the times tables parrot fashion, and chant them out loud right up to twelve times twelve. I even remember reading Shakespeare, though we hadn't a clue what that was about.

Stan Dyer, born 1925

Always the Gooseberries

In those days, there was a terrific class distinction. The real gentry were nice, but it was what they called the middle classes who looked down on the working class. I'll give you an example. At the top of The Park, there was a lady who ran a big market garden. During the summer, she'd employ two or three people from school. She used to pay us three farthings a pound for peas and gooseberries – and Oh! you got scratched picking those gooseberries. Then you'd get a penny farthing for the strawberries. Three of us went one year. My best friend and I went to the Baptist Chapel, but the other girl went to the parish church. If you went to the parish church you got the best jobs. Needless to say, my friend and I always got the gooseberries and the peas.

May Vick (née Beard), born 1918

The Soup Kitchen

One thing I remember about Church Cottage, we had such a lovely big kitchen and, Saturday mornings, a lot of bread used to arrive from Nailsworth, and two gentleman used to come. I think one was an overseer. All this bread was put on our kitchen table, and some scales, and then the poor people used to come – people with big families. According to the size of their family, they had so much bread or a little money, perhaps just a couple of shillings. My mother always used to say, 'Now children, you must not talk about this when you're out because it's just the poor people who are having this bread and this money'.

Now there was a lovely big house called The Lammas, and the Miss Bayneses lived there. They used to have a free library. We used to love to go there and get the books: the *Boys' Own* paper and the *Girls' Own* paper and the *Quiver* and various other things. They also sold milk, and we used to get a quart of skimmed milk for one penny. And it was lovely milk because it wasn't skimmed like it is today, all the cream taken off. And sometimes, when we used to lift the can, the penny was left underneath. We were so thrilled with that. The Miss Bayneses, they were such good people, and

Eva Kirby as a little girl.

they used to have a kind of soup kitchen, and send round soup to people that were ill. They were very very kind.

Now we had some almshouses in the West End. There were eight rooms – one for each old lady. I remember my aunt used to take me to see one of these dear old ladies. Her name was Jane Davies, and she only had one leg. She was always in bed, but she had such a lovely face. And when I was a little girl, I used to think she looked like the Virgin Mary.

Eva Kirby, born 1896

The three lovely Kirby girls – Eva, Jessie and Mary.

The last Nailsworth Urban District Council, in April 1974. Alan Denman is pictured back row, second from left.

Fun Down the Trench

I was working in Shepton Mallet when I applied for the post of Surveyor and Chief Public Health Inspector at Nailsworth Urban District Council. One of my colleagues said to me, 'That's a good place to go – little Switzerland'. It was a very pretty place in those days.

The council offices were opposite Chamberlains in George Street – the big stone building by the cattle grid. There was an outside loo used by all the staff, with a key that you had to get to use it!

Our depot, when I arrived, was a wooden building in a field where the bus station is

Two views of Nailsworth as it was – or 'Little Switzerland' as it was known by some.

now. There was a no-through road from Spring Hill, with a parking area, and the rest was fields and gardens. Lionel Johnson agreed we could buy the old brewery in Brewery Lane, and that became our depot. The building had what was called 'the right of water' which meant we weren't charged water rates.

Leslie Newman was the council foreman, and he was a real character. The first time I met him he said, 'Hello Boss!' which is what he always called me.

I said to him, 'Perhaps you could show me a bit of the district?' so off we went in his car. When we got back to the office, I paid him some kind of compliment about his work and he said, 'Oh my God!' He went over to the wall where he had three dates scribbled down that went back about ten years. He said, 'That's when I've had compliments before'.

He always went everywhere in his car, and wherever he went he turned the car round so it faced the town. It took me a month or two to realise why – he was a retained fireman, and he wanted to be able to get back to the fire station at the bottom of Spring Hill as fast as possible. They didn't have bleepers so there was a siren that sounded at the station when they were needed.

In my time, we culverted Cossack Square and, one day, Leslie was down in the trench, supervising. As I came along I could hear raucous laughter from the men, and there were some women shouting at them. It turned out that every time Leslie was down in the trench, he would tell the women passing by the colour of their knickers! It was all in good fun, though, and the women knew exactly how to take him.

The council had an old road-roller, which was really a museum piece. One day Leslie was surfacing Chestnut Hill and he turned it over. He damaged his pelvis, but even then he was very lucky. If that had fallen on top of him… After that, I persuaded the council to buy a proper, modern roller.

Leslie always kept a pig at the bottom of his garden in Park Road, which he sold to Hilliers. He was a good gardener, and he had a wonderful collection of old troughs that he'd picked up over the years.

Alan Denman, born 1921

Being Over Thirteen

Miss Blick, a lady who kept a shop in Box, once told me that she started work at Evans, a cloth firm in Brimscombe, when she was twelve. Every morning until she was thirteen, she had to go and see the foreman, and he would write '13' on her shoe. He wrote it so that, when the inspector came, she could say to him 'I am over 13', and she would be telling the truth.

Vera Harvey (née Smith), born 1934

Post on a Silver Salver

Mum had rheumatoid arthritis and, as it set in, she couldn't walk at all. I remember her gradually not being able to get about. I used to help do the shopping and get the meals. I think the neighbours did all our washing for us. My father had already died when mum was taken into a nursing home in Cheltenham. I saw her regularly – I went to Cheltenham by bus.

I was fourteen then, and I was sent to the convent in Woodchester – I was there for two years. It was lovely, and I was so happy.

We had to get up at 6.30 in the morning, wash with cold water, and then we went to Mass before we could have our breakfast. They were the Dominican nuns, all dressed in black and white, of course, and I can recall one who was very pretty indeed.

It was a sort of boarding school at the convent. Girls went from about ten until seventeen. A nun came who was more on the modern side when I arrived, and she introduced a uniform that was pale blue blouses and gymslips.

When I'd finished my education, I went to the laundry for a bit. I was in the offices, doing office work and seeing that all the clothes were put in the right piles.

I was taken away from the convent by a friend of my mother's who said she'd keep an eye on me. She had me for a fortnight, then she arranged for me to go into service. I went to Mr Newman at Chestnut Hill House in Nailsworth. He was a bachelor who'd made his fortune in the gold mines of South Africa. I was a house parlourmaid – we had two, and we had a lady housekeeper, Mrs Mirams. She was in the dining room part, and she had two little daughters who lived in the house with her. Those were the days when you took a telegram or a letter in on a silver salver. We would never hand it to Mr Newman directly.

We had a chauffeur and four gardeners – there were beautiful gardens, out of this world. We had a girl on loan from Wills in Bristol – the tobacco people. She stayed with us for a year or two while the Wills were abroad, and she trained me to cook. We did all sorts – beef and chickens – and we cooked dinner parties. The lady housekeeper did all the shopping. When I was house parlourmaid, the uniform was navy blue with a little white 'pinny'. But

Kathleen Sawyer's boss, Arthur Newman (left), with an unknown friend outside Chestnut Hill House, his home which he bought from the Clissold family who had lived there for many years previously.

Kathleen Sawyer (wearing medal, far right hand side) at school with the Dominican nuns at Woodchester.

when I was a cook, they didn't mind what you wore. I generally used to put on an overall. The other maid and I had a bedroom each at the top of the house, and we shared a bathroom between us. I had one half-day off a week, and every other Sunday, and I got five shillings a week.

Mr Newman was very nice. He was in his forties when he came back to England, and he was always very smart-looking. He looked severe, but he wasn't like that at all. He wasn't a gentleman who was a humorist, but one morning he said to me, 'I think I would like a boiled egg'. I said, 'It won't take a minute', and he said, 'Kathleen, I like mine done three to four minutes!'

We'd serve breakfast up in a beautiful silver salver in the morning, with hot water underneath. There'd be bacon, tomatoes,

kidneys, all sorts of things like that. Mr Newman would have breakfast about half past eight, or earlier if he was going to golf. Lunch was at one, and you had to ring the gong at 12.45. The evening meal was half-seven to eight.

Mrs Mirams would come into the kitchen every morning and arrange the menus. She'd be in charge of the flowers in the house, and the drawing room dusting.

We had lots of important people visit us there. The Ballantines used to come – he was a Provost up in Scotland, and he and his sister gave me Scottish blankets for a wedding present that I still use on the bed today.

Down in Nailsworth by Chamberlains, there was a lovely store, Fryers, that sold the most wonderful coffee and farm butter. They ground the coffee while you waited, a half-pound or a pound, and I used to have my own percolator. The coffee was quite expensive. Shopkeepers would always bring up your shopping. You could ring the butcher's up for half a pound of liver and they'd deliver it the same morning.

I used to spend my half-day off with Ted's family when I was courting. They lived where I live now, up the Bath Road. I always had to be back by ten o'clock. I got married in 1931 in Shortwood Chapel – it's Christchurch now – and it was a double wedding, the first they'd had there. We were married on the same day as Ted's sister, and she and I wore the same dresses. We bought them in Bon Marché in Gloucester. We just had a day to choose them. They were long with a bow across the back, and I think they were about £2 10s each. My husband and Harry had their suits made at Burtons in Nailsworth, and there was enough material left over to dress a little pageboy.

Some friends of ours in Bristol lent the four of us their house for a week. We had a lovely time, having meals out and going to the theatre.

I still carried on working at Chestnut Hill House, but Ted and I moved into half the house I live in now, with his dad's aunt living in the other.

Kathleen Sawyer (née Locke), born 1909

Happy and Glad at Kosiclad

I began working for Kosiclad, down in Dunkirk Mills, in 1941. They were a clothes wholesaler who bought from places like Swann and Rowley of Leicester. They were a London firm from EC2. I worked in the invoice department and then the counting house.

The managing directors were Mr Taylor and Mr Stigwood. Mr Taylor was a local gentleman, but Mr Stigwood lived in Cinderford. He used to wear a bowler hat and carry a big umbrella. He came in on Mondays, Wednesdays and Fridays, and you'd see him getting off the Gloucester bus.

Mr Stigwood had a lovely grandson, and they dressed him in the clothes. They used to have posters hanging round the outer office, with rhymes. I remember one said:

The boy in this picture
Is happy and glad.
The reason is simple –
He's Kosiclad.

Vera Skone (née Clark), born 1927

It Shouldn't Happen to a Vet

A lot of the older farmers will remember Tommy Margarson who was still working when I came to the area in 1967. He was a tiny little man with enormous side-whiskers, who always drove a very large motorcar. He could be seen, not looking over the steering wheel, but looking through it. You would just be able to make out his pair of half-moon spectacles. He would drive in the middle of the road at about twenty miles per hour.

It could be quite a dangerous job when I started. Years ago, we used to have to get in amongst the animals and catch them ourselves – 10 to 12 hundredweight of animal – if we wanted, for example, to test them for TB. Now they run them through a cattle crush so it's much safer. There used to be a lot of injuries. I knew a vet who lost an eye. The cow brought its horn up, poked him, and that was that. They didn't disbud the animals then as they do now, and some of them could have two-foot six of horn on them.

It was something I dreaded. Half the time, they would break out through a rickety gate. One farmer had massive animals – Ayreshires if I remember rightly – and we literally had to get in there and capture each one.

Rex Palmer and I started the practice in June 1967, operating for some months from a caravan in his garden in Bowbridge Lane, while the original premises at Bowbridge were being built. No sooner had we started the practice than an outbreak of foot and mouth started in the October with a number of cases the other side of Cheltenham.

While still in the caravan, we were operating on an injured swan to amputate its wing when the anaesthetic must have started to wear off. The swan gave one massive flap of its wing and we ended up with blood sprayed all over the walls and the ceiling of the caravan, which took hours to remove. However, the swan made a full recovery.

There were a lot of very nice farmers and we became good friends with them. They'd always give us a lot of goodies at Christmas – eggs, bacon, and things like that. I can remember a couple of the farmers proudly saying, 'I haven't slept in a bed other than my own for forty years'. They took no holidays – they were dedicated to their farms.

One of the big changes I've seen is the advent of the mobile phone. If you were on call before, you couldn't go out, and nor could your wife. Someone had to be by the phone all the time. I can remember, thirty-odd years ago, being on call one Christmas when we had snow. All the children were out sledging at Besbury. My children got the sledges out of the garage, but I had to tell them we couldn't go anywhere. I can still see the look of disappointment on their faces.

John Pring, born 1934

Losing a Leg, and Finding Work

My dad, George Ellins, was quite a character. He fought in the First World War and lost a leg. He put his age on to get into the army at sixteen, and he was wounded in France and taken prisoner of war. That was where they amputated his leg. He was left injured in No Man's Land, and it turned gangrenous. While he was lying wounded, a German soldier stole his cigarettes out of his pocket and lit one up, but didn't give dad one. He never forgave him for that. It was a German doctor who operated, and dad couldn't speak highly enough of him.

Meanwhile, my mother had been engaged to a sergeant but he was killed in action. He was called Albert Ayres, and he was from Avening. She always kept a photograph of him in uniform that was out through all my parents' married life.

I don't know how she and my dad met, but he used to like a drink in the Crown, and she was very devout and belonged to the Baptist Chapel. Mum persuaded him to go to the chapel too. One day, he went into the Crown where he had a bill on the slate. He said he wanted to pay it all off, and could he have a lemonade. From then on, he didn't drink at all.

They baptised by immersion at the chapel, but dad had had a bullet that went straight through his face. He was always told he must not swim or submerge because it would damage all the repairs, so he was

George Ellins, pictured on the right.

unable to be baptised in this way, but became a member nevertheless.

My dad was very well known in 'Minch'. When he was older, he would stand down on The Cross and direct the traffic, but he'd get it all wrong! He'd always stop the one that had the right of way. He finally got told not to do it by the police from Stroud.

My dad had just a stump of a leg left, so he wore a full-length metal artificial one. There was always a spare one kept in our bedroom, and, going to bed with candlelight, I can remember it used to look a bit spooky. It had a bending knee and foot, and belts that went round the waist and the shoulder to hold it on. I didn't realise how heavy it was until he died and I had to pack it up and send it back. He would walk for miles, and he could even vault a five-barred gate. He had a bike

with a fixed pedal – a lot of people didn't realise he had an artificial leg.

When we were babies, it was very difficult for him to find work, and mother went to work as a weaver in Longfords Mill. The odd job dad got would be as a night watchman if there was a hole dug in the middle of the road. There would be a brazier outside the hut, and then oil lamps around the hole, which he would have to keep going.

Later on, when the war started, he worked for a time down at Critchleys. They were making knitting needles and lots of coloured drawing pins to put in maps. We would watch him working sometimes. There was a big stone trough, full of awful-smelling liquid. Then there was a chain conveyor belt, and he would hang the needles on hooks, which would then get dipped into the solution. It was an awful job – very boring and repetitive. He also used to do fire watching at the mill on a weekend during the war – just watching for fires in the area.

Iris Dyer (née Ellins), born 1930

Like Blackpool Rock

My mother, Kate Bick, joined Hilliers in 1916, when she was fourteen. She left to have me in 1936; then she went back in 1939. Colonel Frank, who owned the company, came up and said would she come back because all the men had gone to war.

During the war, it was not unknown for my mum to work in the factory in the day, and do the office work at night. She slept on a chaise lounge down there. My aunt looked after me. My uncle always said to my mum, 'If they cut your veins open, they'd find 'Hilliers' written there like the lettering in Blackpool rock!'

Mum continued working there, but early in the '50s, she spent a lot of time in hospital with eye trouble. One year she spent eight months out of twelve off ill, but she was still paid full wages.

I used to go and visit her at work sometimes when I was little. It was a very dark, old-fashioned office with big roll-top desks. Mum was secretary to Colonel Frank at that time. She said the only two jobs she never did were 'sticking' the pigs and washing out the chitterlings.

Colonel Frank Evans was a charming man who was good to his workers. Mum always said that his dad, who was known as the 'Old' Colonel, was lovely too, so I suppose

Jackie Porter's mother, Katherine 'Kate' Bick, at work at Hilliers in the 1940s.

Jackie Porter's mum, Kate Bick, is easy to spot on this 1920s Hillier's outing, as her hat flopped in the rain!

his son was a chip off the old block. He had the farm at Sugley in Horsley, that Bunny Arkle bought afterwards. There was always complete respect from the management for the people in the factory. They appreciated the fact that the workers knew their job.

When the pigs were brought to the factory, they came off the lorries and were put into pens. Then the pigs were stunned by electric stunners, which were put either side of their heads. A rope was put round their back legs, and they were hauled up into the air. A huge knife would be put into the jugular vein – 'sticking' – and the pigs would bleed to death into a reservoir underneath.

One time, they hauled a pig up, and the man with the knife went to 'stick' the pig, but the pig's nerves made its front legs jump. The knife went into this man's face, and he was badly cut. My mum was first aider, and she came home absolutely traumatised by this. Her first aid training was very basic, learned when she was with the ARP in the war.

After they were 'stuck', the pigs went on an electric conveyor belt to be gutted. Then they went into a scalding tank to clean them, and a burner to burn off all the hairs. Then someone would scrape them, before the general process of cutting them up.

We'd hear the pigs squealing quite a lot, but you got acclimatised to it. We used to say that the only thing Hilliers didn't use was the squeak!

Pigs came from a very wide area – a forty or fifty-mile radius. But the majority were local, and were brought in by Vivian Young, the transport company, which used to be at Brimscombe. In the early days, they were just driven up on foot.

A lot of people used to keep one or two pigs in their gardens themselves, and, as long as they got them to the factory, Hilliers would kill the pig and butcher it for them. The fee was half the pig.

There was always a ministry man and a council man there for every kill to make sure things were done properly. Pigs aren't stupid – they can smell the blood, so they know what's coming. The drivers had an electric shock device, which they used to poke the pig along. Once one of the drivers kicked a pig that wouldn't move, and Mr Wilson, one of the directors at the time, was really angry. He told the driver that it was cruel to the pig, and it bruised the meat. He phoned the haulier and reported the man.

I started working at Hilliers in 1952, at sixteen. My mum was there, so I went too. It was as simple as that. Whole families worked there together and, in the early days, if you got a job at Hilliers you were very lucky. People didn't leave.

I started as a telephonist and a filing clerk. The bacon was smoked in part of the factory by the offices. It was rather a nice smell of wood burning with the faint aroma of bacon.

The bacon sides were put on beams over the sawdust room. The sawdust, which we got from Workman's timber yard in Woodchester, was lit, and it smouldered. There were no restrictions on us office people going into the factory. If you needed to speak to someone there, you just went down without putting overalls or hairnets on. You just had to watch you didn't slip. The kill area was tiled, and the rest just concrete, and it was washed down every day after the kill.

The standard was always kept very high. I can remember someone claiming to have found a match in a black pudding once, but I really don't know how it could have got there. The chaps on at the time said they only wanted the butt end and they could have had a smoke!

When mum and I moved out of Horsley into Nailsworth, we lived over Hilliers shop in Market Street. It was a flat, and we paid 18s 6d a week. That was a lovely shop. The hams were all hung up in the window, and they always did a beautiful display of all the meats and pies. Mr Frank James was the manager of that shop, and Hilliers had three others in Stroud, Dursley and Cheltenham.

Jackie Porter (née Furley), born 1936

Swan Neck Toilets

One of my biggest responsibilities was supervising Hilliers. Two of us had to be at every kill, and they did five days a week of the kill. It was very modern for that time – all automated. I only ever saw possibly two better-automated factories – Bowyers in Wiltshire, and Walls in London.

Alan Denman pictured in a Lancaster in 1944, during his time in the RAF as a pathfinder/navigator.

Tom Turk was the foreman, and in charge of production. He appeared very laid-back, but he had the confidence of the management and the men. Everything ran smoothly. Colonel Evans was chairman, and there was his son there too, Michael Evans. Michael used to live at The Lawns, now Winslow House. They always had the Conservative fêtes there.

Chamberlains was the other big employer in my area. Teddy Chamberlain was a real gentleman, and he lived in the big house on Pensile Road, which had a tremendous garden, and tennis courts. He contacted me in the early days and said, 'If you have a problem with the factory, come and see me'. If I had an appointment with him, he wouldn't come to the council office. He invited me into his office, in the boardroom in High Beeches. He'd always offer me a drink.

One day, I went to him about a problem I had. Chamberlains had a bit of a tip on the right hand side of Avening Road, and I started to get complaints about it. Teddy Chamberlain said, 'Let's have a look'. So we got into his Bentley, and off we went. After we'd looked round, he said, 'We'll go and have a think about this'. So we went to the Weighbridge to think about it. It's how things were done then. We agreed on trees to screen it so, as soon as the planting season came, trees were planted. They were badly damaged by the terrible snow in the April of 1963.

Chamberlains was Dickensian – it was so old-fashioned and dark. The mill used chemicals and a heavy press method to convert old newspaper into shoe stiffeners. The stream running through was occasionally blood-red, purple or black.

Billy Guy was the Company Secretary, and he was a councillor, and he was always on about footpaths and street lighting

A group of workers outside Chamberlains, date unknown.

because so many of his men walked to work. For that reason, he was backed up by Hilliers. One day, he said that Chamberlains had altered their shift and they were having to walk home in the dark, so we had to alter the street lighting times.

My secretary once told me that some of the factory owners fixed the wages so that they didn't compete with each other. Whether that was true or not, I don't know.

Another working mill – grinding corn – was Egypt Mill, which was owned by Mr Beaufoy King. He lived in a house at the bottom of Tetbury Lane in Bath Road. I went to the mill once and said, 'Where's your toilets?' A workman, G.H. King was the manager, and he said, 'If you haven't seen those, you haven't lived!' He took me to the edge of the stream, and there was a wooden hut with a bar that went straight into the stream. I'd seen them once before like that in Shepton Mallet, and they were called 'swan neck' toilets there. Before my time, Saunders had a small slaughterhouse in Old Market, and all of that went into the stream.

We tested the water coming out of the spouts in places like Watledge, and we found B-coli, which is a pointer to sewage pollution. Most were polluted, and we had to put up notices saying it wasn't drinking water.

Alan Denman, born 1921

Neat as a Pin

When I was fourteen, I left school and got a job through some people my father knew at the pin factory at Frogmarsh. It was all automated. It started off with a coil of brass wire on a big holder. The machine pulled it through and put a head on it. Then it chopped it off to the right length, before it came through a chute, and it was ground off at the point. Each machine made a bucketful of pins a day, and there were about 200 machines in the shop. It was worth seeing.

Perkinson Marmont owned it – that was a family who lived at Woodchester. They used to walk round sometimes, and you had to be on your toes when they did. Mind you, you had to watch it anyway because the foreman, Mr Rigsby, was a disciplinarian.

I worked with him and an apprentice, and we looked after about twenty machines. You'd get bent pins or squashed ones, and you had to make sure the machines weren't turning out deformed pins. The mill shut down in the 1930s.

Later I worked at Mill Bottom Mill – or Ruskin Mill as it's now known. Frank Hender had a little engineering place there doing brass turning, all driven by a water wheel. He was a gentleman, and he was one of the fellows who always had a smart car – a Riley. He was the talk of the town. He was a shortish chap, thickset and he always wore a cap. He lived at Barn's Close.

The company I worked for made shoe stiffeners like Chamberlains. The press came down on my little finger one day and broke it. I went to Stroud Hospital where they were supposed to set it, but it's always been bent since. In the army, they said they couldn't set it again because it might be permanently straight if they did.

Herby Creed, born 1917

Forward-Thinking Women

My mum was christened Constance but she was never called that – her London relatives and friends called her Bibs, because she always wore a bib when she was little. When she came to meet dad, her name was Constance Williams, so she was always called Billy, even by dad.

Before she married, about the time of the First World War, she worked in a grocer's shop. Someone came into the shop one day and asked her to be a sales rep, so she went on the road selling Reckits Blue, which were cubes to put in the rinse after boiling your whites. She said one day she had to go to Harrogate to a conference, and she was the only woman there. She was quite strong-willed.

She was a wonderful mother, very clever. She was a lovely cook, and very proud of her home. We always had meals together as a family – breakfast, dinner and tea. Dad came

'Billy' Bruton, *during her days as a sales rep.*

back for each one. We children were disciplined from day one, and we had to behave. No elbows on the table!

Dad inherited the ironmonger's from his mother. Her family were blacksmiths under the name of Joseph Smith. Strangely enough, Granny Bruton started the ironmonger's with her brother, Uncle Joe, when it became uneconomical to make nuts and bolts and nails. It was cheaper to buy them from Birmingham. Her husband, William, was a partner in a gentlemen's outfitters, where Yarnolds used to be.

Their first ironmonger's premises were next to Prices Store, where the car park is now by the Co-op. Prices was a big grocer's with a storeroom by the side of it, and that's where she started her shop.

I have a bureau in the hall given to Granny Bruton by the Conservative Association. She was quite a worker.

Dorothy Blair (née Bruton), born 1921

All Grist to the Mill

My father-in-law, Alf Harvey, worked at Tommy Harris's mill at Holcombe on the Avening Road. They were the people who used to make flock mattresses out of old clothes and rags. The workers had to pick over the old clothes first – and that was an absolute bonus. It was often men's clothes, such as waistcoats – and sometimes they'd find coins, cigarette cards, penknives, or even the odd 10-shilling note in the pockets. My father-in-law got quite a coin collection that way. Then the clothes were washed, shredded and compressed, and made into stuffing for mattresses for beds.

Vera Harvey (née Smith), born 1934

Harris Mill's outing to Cheddar in the early 1920s. Alf Harvey is third from the left.

Making the Foreman's Breakfast

I went to Longfords in 1946 and worked there until 1952, and then I was sent to London. I got back to them in '64/65, by which time our whole world had changed.

Before I arrived, they employed 160 people to make 60 pieces of cloth. When I retired, we were 120 making 300 pieces a week.

There was a chap there who had started work at Longfords in about 1914. He'd had two jobs then – one was to light the fire for his foreman's breakfast, and the other was to keep the twigs away from the inlet where the water came from the lake. He was called Elijah Glastonbury, and he lived in Avening.

Tom Blackwell was the mill engineer. He was an incredible man – he could do anything. He'd work with wood and metal. A lot of the machines were made of wood, and he'd have to do jobs such as fitting wooden cog wheels. For some reason, when he left, the new mill engineer tore up all the plans of where the pipes went. We were in a real mess. We didn't know if pipes were hot, cold or steam. We ended up having to drill holes in them to find out. They were historic documents that he destroyed.

They were hard conditions at Longfords. For example, there were sets of mules on separate floors, and people were always carrying yarn up and down stairs. It wasn't planned – it had evolved. In 1952, we built a new spinning shop, and then everything was under one roof.

We used to have a barrow for carrying cloth around. Someone once said, 'That's the old fish cart'. Of course, I asked what they meant by that. Apparently, the Playne family used to send a chap down to Nailsworth with this barrow to collect fish from the station, and trundle it back. It was just fish for their own personal use. This cart was still in use in the 1970s.

Our workers came from Avening, Minchinhampton, Tetbury, and, when we wanted more people, from Malmesbury. There were a few from Nailsworth, but Chamberlains were the big employers there. Most people either walked or bussed in. I was told that, in the 1930s, Bill Playne would ride his horse to the mill and hitch it up there.

When I started in '46, there were about five cars among the staff. By the time I became general manager, I had to look around frantically for more car parking space. I became Managing Director in 1982.

Tony Wilson, born 1919

Running the Drying Machine

I went to Central School until I was fourteen-and-a-half. Then my father asked me if I would like to go to Longfords because they had a vacancy there – they wanted someone in the office. I had an interview, and I started the same day, in 1923. Mr Partridge was my manager. He lived in Nailsworth. He wasn't too bad – he was the old-fashioned sort. My job was to run around, and to do book keeping. My hours were 8a.m. until 5.30p.m., and I got 10s, which wasn't a bad wage. I eventually became a director.

The Playnes lived at Longford House, close to the mill. William Playne was the boss, and he had a son and a daughter. His son was wounded in the First World War.

A group of Longfords workers in the early 1920s, including Ethel Heiron (bottom left), mother to Vera Harvey who has contributed to this book.

Mr Playne used to own all the cottages at the Weighbridge, and a lot of workers lived there. There were about 150 workers in the mill when I first went.

My dad was a perfect gentleman. He learned to drive a taxi for a man in Amberley to Stroud station, and I expect he was one of the first round here to do that. He knew Mr Yeo, and he was in charge of Longfords at that time, so Mr Yeo got him a job at Longfords when his taxi job finished.

My dad worked at the drying. A lot of water was used in cloth, and it had to be dried. They had a drying machine, run by steam, and the cloth ran in between pipes. His job was to guide the cloth onto the spikes to keep it going round.

Mr Yeo was very strict. He never missed a thing and, if there was anything wrong, he saw it and he let you know. The conditions in the mill were good. It wasn't cold – there was steam-heating all the way round in pipes.

All the cloth was taken every day by horse and cart to the station, and the coal was fetched back for heating and driving the turbines.

I never knew an outing arranged by Longfords, but in about 1930 the workers got together to go to Weston for the day. We went by charabanc, the kind with solid tyres.

I was conscripted to stay in my job at Longfords during the Second World War. We were making uniforms, and cloths for sealing petrol tanks. If the petrol tanks were hit by a bullet, the cloth sealed it up, and they didn't lose so much petrol. We lost a lot of young people to the war, and so we employed West Indian people. We had them in Springhill House that we owned. There were eight of them in there. We trained them to do the jobs to take the place of the

Stan Dyer at Phoenix, in around 1949.

men who'd left. They were about twenty to forty years old, and they got on all right, but they kept themselves to themselves. A lot of women took the place of weavers.

Ivor White, born 1908

Don't Go to the Foundry!

In 1940, when I was due to leave school, a man from the Labour exchange came round. He was only interested in getting boys into munitions factories, so I was guided into engineering. My dad's only comment was 'Tell him you don't want to go into the foundry'.

I got an apprenticeship at the Phoenix Iron Works in Thrupp. They did work for the Admiralty, making compressors for submarines

Stan Dyer's father, George, at his retirement presentation in 1956.

and frigates. That was one of Blake's Dark Satanic Mills. It was filthy. There were no washing facilities – just a standpipe in the yard with cold water. You got filthy working there. There was a lot of cast iron moulding that gives off dust. I must have breathed in tons of it. I know two boys who lost an eye. Bobby Ford had a bit of metal fly off the machine and hit him in the eye. Arthur Herbert was another one. You got no wages or compensation. If you were ill, you just didn't get paid. Apprentices worked a forty-eight-hour week. At fifteen, my first wage packet was 8s 6d from which they deducted 2d for the hospital fund. I handed it over to mother and got sixpence back for myself.

Stan Dyer, born 1925

Brass Foundry in Brewery Lane

My father came to Nailsworth with his family from Bradford in about 1908. My grandfather started up a brass foundry in Brewery lane called J.H. Hartley and Son. Subsequently, my grandfather went to Newman and Hender as foreman of their brass foundry, and my father took over Brewery Lane. Grandfather had a big, wax moustache, and grandmother was severe-looking, but she wasn't like that really. She was very tall, with white hair.

Then, when my grandfather died in 1936, my father took over his job at Newman and Hender. My dad always came home for a midday meal. He caught the bus to get there, but a lot of people did walk.

I can remember going down to the Brewery Lane foundry on one occasion, when my father was operating it. You poured the molten metal from a crucible, and I recall standing on one side and helping him pour it in. That wouldn't be allowed nowadays! The actual foundry was very small, and backed on to Johnsons. My father did work for Chamberlains, among others. As he had a motorbike, he could go out and get work from quite a distance. He used to go out to a firm called Gordons – about twenty miles away – that made pumps.

Wilfred Hartley, born 1922

Terrible, Dirty Work

I was on the Labour a fortnight – getting 7s a week – before I was sent to Newman and Hender in the foundry. It was terrible, dirty work. You got filthy dirty. There were sulphur fires, and you couldn't see across the room sometimes. We went home pretty black.

I saw a bloke had his arm ripped out. Sometimes the belt would come off the wheels on the shaft, and men would put the belt back on with their hand, with it still running. That was a lazy way of doing it, and they weren't supposed to. There were no medical people on the premises, so they

George Waller's Phoenix Iron Works in Thrupp, in the mid-1930s.

Norman Vick (on left) helping to build the stone church at Box. The old tin church it replaced is clearly visible inside.

took him to Stroud. He came back to work eventually, but he'd lost his arm.

Other men would have to pour white hot metal – they were the hand moulders. The metal came out of the furnace in a big pot. There would be a man either side, each holding a handle, and they'd pour it into the mould.

I used to offer to make three fellows' tea so that I could keep a bit of tea and sugar from each one to make my own! I didn't tell them, and so everyone was happy.

I spent many years in the building trade before finishing up at Chamberlains on maintenance. I was always on call, but we didn't have a phone. So the van would come round if there was a problem. We'd hear it coming up the street at two o'clock in the morning sometimes, and I'd have to get up and go and see what was wrong.

Norman Vick, born 1914

Basins Don't Bounce

My dad worked at Newman and Hender. When I was a child, I used to go down with his dinner in a white pudding basin with a cloth over the top. Mum would cook a hot meal for him, and I'd take it down through Forest Green to the factory. One day, one of the local boys said to me, 'Drop it and see how it bounces'. So I dropped it and it broke!

Kathleen Sawyer (née Locke), born 1909

Winning on Littlewoods

I left school at fourteen, and I went to the stocking factory, Walkers, at Dunkirk Mills. There used to be the Walkers stick factory next door. We made men's socks out of cotton. I had eight machines to look after. It was only piecework, but it was a lot of fun. The factory was the first time I'd had a flush toilet. It was a bucket toilet at home. My mum dug a hole, thoroughly limed it, disposed of the bucket, limed it all again, and then put soil on the top of that.

In those days, we were very poor, but when I got married I used to go on the Littlewoods coupon for 1s 7d. One day, my sister checked my coupon on the Saturday night and she said, 'You've won some money!' We were so excited. I won £370, which they sent in the post, and I bought my own home at Windsoredge.

It was a lot of money. I'd been working at Hilliers for sixpence an hour until ten o'clock at night. It was dirty, hard work, washing chitterlings. Later I learned to do the skins for sausages.

When it was wartime, my foreman Mr Frank Pinnel, said he was short-staffed, and he wanted me to work with the men. He sent me into Hilliers office for a stunner, which was like a gun. I had to help pull the rope around the animals' heads to get them down. The eyes would nearly come out. I often think back to how cruel it was, but if your foreman told you to do something, you didn't have the choice. Mr Harry Grant was the butcher.

When I had my children, I went potato picking every year at Mr Bertram King's farm half way up to Nympsfield. I used to take my children, and they could take two or three potatoes home to have for tea. It was very badly paid, but we loved doing it.

Muriel Newman (née Davis), born 1916

CHAPTER 5

War

Sylvia Dyer, now Phelps, at home, with her dad, and pet dog (see p. 98).

(see p. 98)

Hiding in the Cupboard

When the war broke out, we came from London to live here permanently, and mother got us into Cheltenham College. On the first day of the war, there was a warning, and I made the whole family hide in the cupboard under the stairs. It became too hot in the end, so we came out.

After the bombing of Bristol, we could see the town burning. It was a red glow, and we just thought how awful it all was. German bombers had an extremely distinctive sound – a sort of broken noise. You could hear them flying over to bomb Bristol, but you just got used to them. I can also remember all the signposts being removed in this area.

There was a signal that if the church bells were rung, we all had to get ready for invasion. One day, all the church bells rang. Arthur from the farm got his pitchfork and rushed up to Minchinhampton, followed by us. Nothing happened. It was a false alarm!

My mother took in a Dutch Jewish girl called Ann Bekenhaupt. She had been evacuated onto a ship, which was then sunk. She was thrown into the water, and she watched her parents drown. She was very disturbed. I remember her always being hungry, and as thin as a rake. Bread wasn't rationed in the war – only afterwards – and mother used to buy loaves of bread, put them in the oven and make crispy toast. I can see Ann wandering around eating this toast.

We went out one day, towards the end of the war, and found that the Common was a sheet of white tents. It was American soldiers camped there – and they were all black because, in those days in America, they were segregated. We'd never seen black people before.

Lady Mary Rawlinson (née Hill), born 1923

Wonderful Negro Spirituals

During the war, one summer's evening, a camp appeared with 900 black personnel and 10 white officers. The Park had all the white Americans.

These coloured servicemen were in trouble – I don't know what they'd done – and they were forbidden to write home. Lots of them got different people in the village to post letters for them. They were nice young fellows.

One or two were allowed to go into 'Minch'. They were walking down the street, when they asked a local person, 'Excuse me, Lady, will you tell me where the post office is?' Coming up the street were two white Americans in uniform. They said to this local person, 'Were they hassling you, Lady?' We saw first-hand the aggression there was from the whites.

When these black servicemen arrived, their supplies hadn't caught up with them. They had no water and very little food. They went up to The Park and asked their own personnel for food, and they were refused. Local people gave them things for the three or four days before their food came. And remember, at this time we were well into food rationing.

They invited Mr Brooks, who ran the chapel in Box, to go and take a service with them. He said to them, 'If any of you want to come to our service, you can'. When he looked round, he had three or four hundred people following. Mr Hopper stood out on the bank, relaying the service to them. The singing was wonderful. They chose the hymn, *When the roll is called up yonder* and other Negro spirituals.

These young men went across the Channel and took a pounding. A big percentage didn't make it home. They could only have been nineteen or twenty years old.

In the wartime, you were only allowed to paint your home brown or green, camouflage colours. Mr Brooks lived in a caravan in a field at the top of Scar Lane. It was wooden and inscribed with evangelic text all over it. The authorities told him he couldn't live in it unless he painted it all over, but he wouldn't. So he was allowed to move it to the quarry up the Horsley Road where it could be hidden behind bushes.

Vera Harvey (née Smith), born 1934

Sylvia Dyer (now Phelps) in her Girls' Training Corps uniform, on a trip to London.

Sweets for My Sweet

Whenever the American troops came up Burleigh Hill in their lorries, they used to throw us sweets if they saw any of us children. Sweets were rationed, of course, so that was very nice. It was often chewing gum in flat sticks.

The Americans were very fond of the local girls. One gave my friend some sweets and asked a group of us, 'Has anybody here got a sister?' My friend said, 'Yes!' 'Where is your sister?' he asked. 'In her pram', she replied.

Down at Brimscombe, they had the Royal British Legion Club and, on a Saturday, they would have a whist drive followed by a dance. My mother would be behind the counter, helping to do cups of tea, and, as she wouldn't let me stay at home by myself, I would go with her. I can remember one night, one of the black Americans was having a dance with the girl of one of the white Americans. There was an almighty fight, and I had to stand on a chair to keep out of the way. After that, they had to say no black Americans could come to the dance. But, you know, I don't think it was their fault. I don't think the fellow was dancing with someone else's girl on purpose.

Sylvia Phelps (née Dyer), born 1935

Naughty But Nice

I left school when I was fourteen, and mother wanted me to be an apprentice at Morris's in Nailsworth. But the First World War was on, and I had been taught at school to help my King and Country, so I went to munitions at Newman and Hender. A very nice place, that was. We were making the big shells, and they were brass – beautiful to look at.

I can remember all the boys leaving to go to war. I was only fourteen, but all the young girls working there had somebody in the Forces they thought a lot of. A cousin I had went and I used to write letters to him. Both world wars were terrible, but the First was worse, with all the trenches.

There were a lot of parties after the First World War finished. The soldiers were there at Armistice. I can remember, I was working at Newman and Hender at eleven o'clock on Armistice – the first one. We had to wait for the hooter to go, then we all rushed off and went home.

We had rationing in both wars. I have never been hungry, but I know what it's like to have to eat rough brown bread. We were allowed two ounces of butter a week, two of margarine – and cheese, meat and tea were rationed. But you'd be surprised how we got by. In the Second World War, I used to make sponge sandwiches with liquid paraffin. I shouldn't say that because it wasn't really allowed! It was used as fats, and the sandwiches would come up lovely, spread with raspberry jam out of the garden.

Lilian Day, born 1902

No Room For Two

When the Second World War broke out, we took in evacuees. The first lad came from Eastbourne where they had started bombing. He was called Arthur Long and, poor little chap, he looked so down and out.

Winnie Proctor, the land army girl who came for one or two weeks, but ended up practically one of the Sawyer family.

He must have been five or six, and he had a pair of trousers on with no seat. So my husband and I took him down to Yarnolds and rigged him out. The next day, his father and mother arrived and said they had been given a house for the whole family at Windsoredge.

About a week after, a lady said, 'We've got some children from Birmingham. Will you have one?' I said I wouldn't have any more, but she asked me just to go down to the Town Hall. Sure enough, there were these little kiddies there. A lady who lived in the red brick houses opposite, said she would take a little boy called Jimmy. Another lad beside her piped up, 'I want to go with Jimmy!' but she said she couldn't take two. I told him to come with me. His name was Brian Milward, and I told him that I had a son, Peter, who was about his age. He was a bit homesick at first, but he soon settled in. So my husband arrived home to find an extra child, but he didn't

Kathleen Sawyer, in her twenties.

Peter Sawyer, Kathleen's son, (top right hand side of middle pair of boys), at the British School with 'Gaffer' Michael in the late 1930s.

mind. Brian's mum and dad came once a month. She worked in the Cadbury's chocolate factory, and she used to bring all the food she could to help out.

The next thing was, I had my niece from Bristol as well. She arrived out of the blue with her mother in a taxi. They'd had a terrible night because the bombing had started there.

We also had a land army girl. She'd hurt her back on the tractor at Mr Cox's farm at Nupend, so she came for a week or two until she got better. She was called Winnie Proctor and she came from Ilford, London – in the end we decided she should stay too. She had worked as a court dressmaker for Mercers. She'd had the choice of going into the munitions or joining the land army which is what she'd chosen to do. Her dad had said to her, 'I'll give you a month!'

I remember the night the planes went over to Coventry. We heard the zooming coming. It was a beautiful moonlit night

when we watched them go over in threes and sixes. I said, 'Birmingham's going to get it tonight', but it was Coventry so we heard later. My husband said, 'Where are our planes?' and then we heard them roar up in Spitfires from Aston Down.

Kathleen Sawyer (née Locke), born 1909

Working in a Thunder Storm

My father was chief ARP warden during the war. The young men had all gone, so the men who remained were either elderly, or worked on the land. I was teaching by then, but I used to work at the local farm in the school holidays, driving tractors and such like. I remember an old man who used to make the most beautiful stooks out of corn trying to teach us how to do it. But we found it impossible to get all the corn stalks in!

We had one very satisfactory day. There

was a thunderstorm coming, and the local farmer asked if we could go on for an extra two hours before the storm arrived, to finish the field. The POWs were only allowed to do a certain number of hours, and the paid labour refused to work on. So it was up to us who were unpaid. We carried on until ten o'clock at night, and got the job done. That was very satisfactory!

Anyone who worked on the land got perks. We got a bread and cheese lunch which was the equivalent of a whole ration for the week – though we needed it. You were also allowed to pick up grain for your hens, which was a great help. Nobody cheated in those days.

For about three months at the end of the war, the Americans were on The Park. They

Gladys Beale, during her teaching days.

were very generous to the children who had a wonderful time while they were there.

One of the saddest things for me is that practically all the boys I taught before the Second World War were killed fighting. Looking at the names in the chapel at Oakley Hall is like looking at a class list.

Gladys Beale, born 1907

'I Can't Choose!'

During the Second World War we had two evacuees – two little girls from Birmingham aged six and eight. A year before war broke out, we were all assessed and asked if we

Maud Elliott, who went on to marry Joe Smith of Woefuldane, wearing the Land Army uniform of the First World War.

would have evacuees. The day came and the billeting officer told my sister she could come and choose two. My sister said, 'I can't choose!' so she was given two that were left. They were two frightened little girls with gas masks round their necks called Pat and Marjorie Thomas. They were wonderful children – obedient, clean, and they fitted in straight away. We had them for four years, and they wrote each week to their parents. The little one would say, 'I don't know what to write!' When she had two lines, she would heave a sigh of relief and say, 'I've wrotten to my mother'.

They'd never seen a cow before. We took them onto the Common and sat Marjorie on a cow, and she went on as happy as Larry. We used to take them down Mundon's Hill into Gatcombe Woods and pick the wild

Noel Playne, pictured top, middle, at 7a.m. after the night shift at the Phoenix munitions factory in the First World War.

strawberries, and the bluebells. After Colonel Ricardo died, R.A. Butler had Gatcombe, and we had to get a permit to go there. I can understand it – people had abused it really.

During the war, I went to work at Tylers of Thrupp first of all. They made gliders for the invasion of France. Then I went to Sperry Gyroscope where we assembled gyroscopes for keeping aircraft level. I didn't like the work – it was so repetitive. We earned good money, though – £2 10s a week. The thing I was dreading was that I should be put into the machine shop. It was underground and very noisy. But I wasn't – I don't think I should have stood that.

We had one day off one week and a half-day off the next. There were two sisters there who were granted not to work on a Sunday for religious reasons. They sent a van out for us on a Sunday because there were no buses. It was like a Black Maria – there were no windows in it. In the winter, we didn't see daylight because it was dark when we arrived and dark when we came home.

Jessie Kirby, born 1909

All Rubber Sheets and Bedpans

I have a picture of my mother, Noel Playne, working during the First World War in what I think was more of a convalescent home in Nailsworth. It was staffed by Red Cross nurses, with one professional sister who was in a plain apron. The more serious cases were probably looked after in Stroud, and came to Nailsworth when they were getting better. Chrysogon Beale was there too. My mother said her main memory of the Red Cross was of emptying bedpans and

Chestnut Hill House, in Nailsworth in around 1915, where soldiers were treated by Red Cross nurses and professional medical staff, during the First World War. Noel Playne is seated – the nurse on the right of the line – with her friend Chrysogon Beale standing behind her.

scrubbing rubber sheets. She left the Red Cross to work in the Phoenix munitions factory run by a Mr Hines – known as Papa Hines – making shell cases.

Anne Woollcombe-Boyce, born 1921

Fabulous Money

I remember when the Boer War was on, and Mafeking was relieved, we had torchlight processions round the town, headed by the band, ending up in The Park with a big bonfire. When the Great War started in 1914, I was dressmaking. We had very little money for it. So one day, I heard they wanted girls on munitions at Quedgeley. My cousin and I, Lucy Sparks, we both had bicycles. We thought we'd make our own minds up that we'd go, because the money was a pound a week which we thought was

fabulous. But, of course, when we got home and I told my uncle about it, he said, 'Oh no! You're not going, and I know Lucy won't go'.

Anyway after a little while, Newman and Hender were advertising, which was much nearer home, so we eventually got a job down there. We had to start at half past five in the morning from Minchinhampton, get in at six o'clock and work till six o'clock at night. The walk was about two miles. We'd come through all the Common, many times in deep snow. As I said, a pound a week – it was the money that attracted us.

Once, when we'd been working all night, we came out and the snow was up to our knees. I never thought I'd get home, but eventually I did, and we went again the next morning and walked all down Nailsworth.

There was no transport in Minchinhampton. If you wanted to go to Stroud, you had to go to Brimscombe Halt

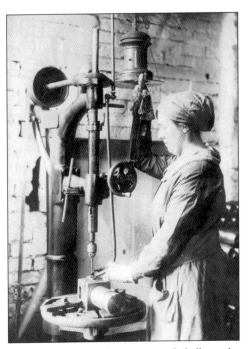

A Miss Godsell drilling 18-pound shells at the Phoenix factory in the First World War.

and get on the railcar. And you could go to Stroud for 4d return, and Gloucester for a 1s return. But, after a while, Mr J. Merritt started two buses, and we could go from Minchinhampton to Avening, Avening to Nailsworth, Stroud, back to Minchinhampton, all the way round, for a shilling, which was a lovely drive.

Kitty Dowding, born 1884

The 'Casuality' List

I don't remember very much about the First World War, but I do remember George Ellins, a native of Minchinhampton, who unfortunately lost his leg in the First World War. He used to come into our house at Church Cottage to clean his buttons on his tunic. This was after he lost his leg. He had a piece of metal – brass – about two to three inches wide, with a slot down the middle, and he used to put the button through this slot and clean it with the Brasso. This was so that it wouldn't mark the material.

I remember my grandfather would come to our house during the war with the daily paper, and he used to sit down in our kitchen and say to my mother 'Now I'll read 'ee the "casuality" list'. And he used to go all through the casualty list and my mother held her breath, because, of course, my eldest brother was in the war. She was quite all right after grandfather got beyond the 'k's and she used to know her son was all right.

Another thing I remember about the war – when I was at school, we used to pick blackberries, which were sent away to some factory to make blackberry jam for the troops. And we were paid a penny a pound for picking them. Of course, it was wonderful if you lived at Burleigh because you were surrounded by blackberry brambles. In fact, a part of the common there was, and still is, called Black Ditch. But I think one of the things that I remember most about the end of the war, was that the Armistice was signed on a Monday. My mother was doing the washing, and she was so excited and so thrilled to think that the war was over, that during her washing she starched the woollen socks.

Jessie Kirby, born 1909

A Lodger For Life

Some of my earliest recollections are of soldiers – strange men in uniform – being in the house. Mum explained they were billeted with us because we had spare bedrooms, and everyone had to do their bit towards the war effort. Dad was 'called up' and was on guard duty on the East Coast, being too old to go overseas.

Sometime during the war, a crippled friend of the Revd Sammy Ford, was anxious to leave London to escape the Zeppelin raids, and mum was asked to shelter him 'for the duration'. However, when the war ended in 1918, John refused to return to London, and made his home with us until his death in 1930. It was John who had – what must have been – one of the first 'cat's whisker' radio sets in Minchinhampton, and I can still remember the thrill of putting on the headphones and hearing 'This is London calling', when I was a little girl.

Looking back, I often wonder how mum coped with a family of four children, a husband and a lodger, and a large house. There were certainly no mod cons. Washdays started early with lighting a fire under the boiler in the kitchen to heat the water, and, when I came home from school in the afternoon, mum would be on her hands and knees scrubbing the red-tiled kitchen floor.

Winifred Glassonbury (née Gardiner), born 1912

The Red Coats

I remember the end of the South African war, when some of the men came back to Minchinhampton. There were three of them, and my uncle was one. They belonged to the Guards, and I remember so well, although I was only a little girl, the red coats they wore.

Now in the First World War, there were

many things to raise money for a Patriotic Fund. Every week, a committee of ladies and helpers used to go to the men's club – it used to be called the gymnasium – and they would cut out shirts, and knit socks and balaclava helmets. My mother made a shirt most weeks all the years that the war was on. I shall never forget the service we had in church on Armistice Day. The church was simply packed. Every time we hear now the hymn *Now thank we all our God*, I shall never forget that service. The people were crying and singing. It was a most wonderful day, when the war ended in 1918.

Eva Kirby, born 1896

Putting Up the Dunkirk Survivors

I was nine years old when war was declared on September 9 1939. It was a Sunday and we had just come home from Chapel at twelve midday. My parents turned the radio on, and we heard the Prime Minister, Mr Neville Chamberlain, telling the nation that we were now at war with Germany. I had understood that it was a very serious declaration, and I remember my mother's reaction of despair at the thought of another war, having gone through the 1914–18 First World War. I had heard the adults talking about it in recent days, and we had a boarder who was in the Army Reserve who had been called up as a reserve lorry driver as war seemed imminent. I remember my mother in tears when we wished him goodbye a few days before.

Soon after the war began, food became rationed because it was too dangerous for our merchant ships to cross the seas to import food, as they could be torpedoed by

enemy submarines or bombed by enemy aircraft. Also, a lot of the merchant ships were commandeered for active service, which meant there was a shortage of ships anyway. There was a 'Dig for Victory' campaign throughout the land, encouraging everyone to dig all their gardens up, including the front lawns and flowerbeds, to grow vegetables, and help feed themselves to supplement the meagre rations.

Our mothers improvised as best they could, and I remember I was quite fond of the dried egg that replaced the fresh eggs. I used to make an omelette, which was quite tasty – that was my Saturday morning breakfast treat! I gave up sugar in my tea to help mum eke out the rations. But I was quite used to drinking tea without sugar. I

was often thirsty when I got home from school, and I would drink my mother's cup of tea. She didn't take sugar anyway, so this was no real hardship on my part.

Another sacrifice I made for the war was when we had a 'War Weapons Week' in 1941 when we were asked to raise money. There was an auction sale under the Market House, and I donated my beloved doll's house. I couldn't bear to go to the sale to see how much it fetched. My mother went and said it raised quite a handsome sum when the auctioneer explained that a little girl had given it.

I remember the evening of June 1940, when a troop of soldiers who were survivors from the beaches of Dunkirk were marched up Tetbury Street and halted just outside the

Institute where I lived. They were exhausted, and only possessed the clothes that they stood up in. Our local policeman, 'Bobby' Buckle was knocking on doors and pleading with our neighbours to take these poor men in for the night. He came to my mother – he knew everyone well in Minchinhampton as he had been our policeman for years – and begged her to help. We didn't have any spare beds, although we had an attic, which was large, clean and comfortable and empty, apart from a few vegetables stored there. A very nice, wealthy neighbour, who lived just a few doors up the street, came running down and said, 'Oh, Mrs Ellins, if you have the room, I can supply the bedding'. So two very tired and worn soldiers came into our house, and then this kind neighbour, a Mrs Alison, sent down two mattresses, sheets, pillow and blankets, one set all pink, and one set all blue. Meanwhile, dad had gone off round to Butt Street and was knocking on doors there asking people to take in as many soldiers as they could for the night, which they willingly did.

Mother cooked for the soldiers their first proper meal for days – we didn't mind sharing our rations at all. They had a bath in the public baths in the Institute (we had no bathroom in the house) and then sank into bed. In the morning, my father took them both a cup of tea to wake them up and, when they opened their eyes and saw where they were, they said they thought they must have died and gone to heaven! They had had a dreadful, terrifying experience on the Dunkirk beaches waiting to be rescued.

After breakfast, they had to parade in the Market Square to be moved on, but, before they went out, every man was given a pair of socks and a packet of cigarettes collected from the people of Minchinhampton during the night. All of the men of that troop were taken in by the kind folk of Minchinhampton that night, and we were so glad they had survived such an horrific ordeal. Our hearts went out to them. Because they were moved on, we only got to know the soldiers' names, and we often wondered how they recovered from their ordeal.

Iris Dyer (née Ellins), born 1930

CHAPTER 6

Leisure

An unknown celebration at an unknown location, but among the group are Minchinhampton revellers.

Hoops and Whip Tops

The games we used to play at school were skipping, and whip tops. That was a marvellous game. You had a stick with a long lash on it, and the tops were like mushrooms, prettily painted at the top. You wound the core round the stem of the whip top, put it under your foot, and pulled the whip away quick – and the top spun. And then you used to whip this top and keep it spinning – for hours, I suppose, if you had time. We also played hopscotch. But this we weren't allowed to do if we had our best shoes on, because mother said we would wear them out. Marbles, we used to play, and 'Onkers', the fruit of the chestnut. An 'onker' used to have a hole bored in it, and a string put through with a knot on the end. It was held up by one person, to be knocked by another person. And the person that won was the one that broke the 'onker'. We were a bit crafty. We found out that, if we put it in the oven and baked it hard, it didn't break quite so easily.

Another of the things we used to play with were hoops. Now the girls' hoops were made of wood, about 20 to 24 inches in diameter. We were supplied with a stick, and we just used to hit this hoop, and it used to bowl down the road. The boys' hoops were a wonderful thing, made of iron. Attached to the hoop was a ring, and attached to the ring was a piece of iron, like an iron stick. And they bowled these hoops with the ring attached. I can't quite explain it, but perhaps you've got enough imagination to know what I'm talking about.

We also went to Sunday School on Sunday mornings, and to the children's service on Sunday afternoons. Saturday nights, my mother used to say to us, 'Have you learnt the Collect for the day?' because that was one of the things that we had to know, the Collect for the Sunday. And we'd say, 'Yes, mother!' hoping that she wouldn't say, 'Well let me hear you say it', because sometimes we really didn't know it.

Christmas, of course, was a wonderful festival for everybody. It always has been and always will be. And about two weeks before Christmas, we used to have a wonderful outing – we used to go to Stroud. We'd go on the railcar from Brimscombe Halt, which ran about five or six minutes past every hour. We were so excited about this outing that we used to start about an hour before it was necessary. We only had to walk down the hill. We went down the little lane called Featherbed Lane. There were three stops in the railcar. We started at Brimscombe and we went to Ham Mill. From Ham Mill we went to Bowbridge and from Bowbridge we went to Stroud. And, do you know, that used to seem like going up to London. It was ever such a long time.

We always had a Christmas tree. Well – yes, it was a Christmas tree, but not like we have now. It was usually a large bough from a yew tree. And it wasn't put up a month or three weeks before Christmas. It was put up on Christmas Eve, after we'd gone to bed, so that it was a great surprise to us on Christmas morning. We didn't have electric lights, but we had candles, real candles on the tree, and we also had Christmas presents, of course. But we didn't know what we were going to have. We didn't ask our parents to buy us what we wanted. We just accepted with grace and thankfulness what they gave us. We had lovely decorations in our house too. We had lovely lanterns – collapsible lanterns – and they had real candles in when they were lit. I don't know what the fire officer would say now if he could see that. And in the window at the back of the house, we had a lantern that looked like a full moon with a face on it, and that had a candle in it too.

I come now to Good Friday. Living in a churchyard as we did, of course all the church festivals were busy times for my father. And there was always the three hours' devotional service on Good Friday from twelve o'clock until three o'clock. To get us out of the way, my father used to take us children into Gatcombe Woods, down The Pieces. The Pieces is a field, Minchinhampton-side of the wood, and it's got a very steep bank. As you stand at the top of this bank, there's a little stream that runs along the bottom. We used to think this was wonderful because it formed the letter "M". We always used to think about that. It's still there, too. We used to go into Gatcombe Woods with a basket or a paper bag, and several pieces of wool, 10 or 12 inches long, and we'd pick primroses and violets for the decoration of the church for Easter Day. And as we picked them, we used to tie them up with these bits of wool, so they would be tidy and save us a lot of work when we got home.

And then we come to Whitsuntide. The main attraction at Whitsuntide, of course, was the fair. We didn't have silly things like spring bank holidays and all the rest of the things that go on these days. Whitsuntide was Whitsuntide. And we didn't have the fair a week or ten days before Whitsun. It used to come on Whit Sunday afternoon. When we were in church at the children's service, we could hear these heavy wagons going up Bell Lane, and we used to nudge each other and say, 'The fair's come! The fair's come!' Poor old Canon Sears. Well, of course, he couldn't contain us. He had to let us out early.

And there were always the Sunday School Whitsuntide treats. The church treat was held on Whit Monday. That was a marvellous affair. We used to have seed cake for tea – caraway seed cake. I always associate that with Whitsunstide treats. And we used to go to The Lammas, and we'd have swings that had been erected in an avenue of trees. We had races and scrabbles for sweets.

On Whit Tuesdays, it was the Baptist Church Sunday School treat. They had a wonderful procession. They used to process all the way round the streets and, in front of their procession, they had a beautiful floral banner, which must have stood ten feet tall, I should think. And it was decorated with the flowers of the season, but mainly I can see it decorated with Golden Chain – laburnum (we didn't call it laburnum in those days) – these lovely golden flowers hanging down, and lilac.

The summer holidays to me were always hot. We never had cardigans when we were children. We just had winter clothes and summer clothes. We spent nearly all our

The floral crown, leading the parade, in Friday Street.

summer holidays in The Park. Mother used to cut us a packet of sandwiches, and we used to take a bottle of cold tea. That was our picnic. Butter and jam sandwiches, I expect it was.

We used to make tents. We'd go into the cellar and find a large piece of sacking, and a pole. We'd stick the pole in the wall, and drape the sacking over it, and that was our tent. I remember once cutting up one of father's potato sacks to be made into a tent. I only did it once, mind! I didn't do it again.

We used to make the outline of houses out of stone. We made them properly. We had the doors and the windows and the kitchens and the bedrooms. And, although we could very easily have stepped over this line of stone to go into the sitting room, we always went in through the door.

Another thing I remember when I was quite young, they used to have a thing called Hospital Sunday. I think this was organised by what is now called the Stroud Benefit Society.

They had a huge procession in the town, headed by the town band, and, incidentally, my father played the drum and the cymbals in the town band. A lot of us girls used to dress up in our Sunday best, and we had baskets, decorated with flowers. We collected loose money in these baskets, and that was all taken to church and blessed and sent to the hospital.

Jessie Kirby, born 1909

The Whitsuntide Treat

The Whitsuntide Treat was always on the Whit Monday. It would start with the decoration of the floral crown, which headed the parade. It was made with lilac

Iris Dyer's mother, Minnie, with her sister Poppy in pram, at a Baptist parade in the 1920s.

and Golden Chain, and we used to decorate it in the graveyard. Meanwhile the ladies were in the Sunday School, making sandwiches and cutting up slab cake in the upstairs room.

In the afternoon, we had to rehearse all the hymns with Avening Band. At three o'clock, we came out of the chapel. The crown, which was on a pole, went first, then the band, then the senior Bible Class, then the Sunday School classes in order, down to the babies on the Cradle Roll. The very newest one would be in a very fancy pram. We would decorate the little primary children in threes, with paper chains tying them together. Then the one who had done the most attendances was put in a decorated

cart and pulled by the teachers.

We went from the chapel, up to the allotments and down Friday Street into the Market Square where we would sing a hymn. Then we would go down to The Cross and sing *All Hail the Power of Jesu's name*. Then we'd go up West End to where it forks, and sing another. Coming down West End, we would sing *Onward Christian Soldiers*. Then down Well Hill, it would be *Jesus Bids Us Shine*. We all had flags of various kinds that we would wave.

Then we went back up to Chapel Lane, outside the Sunday School, where we would sing *God Bless Our School*. Finally, we would all go into Sunday School and have our tea. The little ones would be downstairs, and all the bigger ones upstairs. The band had a free tea.

When the tea was over, someone would produce a handcart and take several of the forms and put them in The Park where Roger's Fun Fair was, and we would race

for money and listen to the band. If you won, you got ninepence. The cows in The Park would gradually move down and listen to the music. They were quite taken with it.

When we paraded round the streets, we would get hundreds of visitors. Sightseers would come from Chalford, Hyde, Brimscombe, Burleigh, Box, Avening, Nailsworth – it was a big thing. Then there was Rogers Fun Fair. The fair would always give a donation to the church, and they would never start the fair until we had paraded through.

Mr Rogers's caravan was always dark red and the biggest. It was beautiful. Even their water cans were polished brass. The windows in the caravan were patterned with frosted glass and scrolls. They used to come from Crackstone where they parked overnight. They would come down Butt Street and up Bell Lane when they arrived. They had the old-fashioned traction

The 1914 Baptist Sunday Shool treat and, later (below), the same parade reaches the High Street.

engines with smoke coming out of the chimney. We'd be in school, but we'd hear them coming, and there would be such great excitement.

Iris Dyer (née Ellins), born 1930

Last In Is The Winner!

Nailsworth swimming pool was in the pond beyond Lock's Mill. It belonged to Mr Johnson who had the engineering works, and he gave it to the town to use. It was fresh water, and the Horsley stream ran through it. They had a swimming club, with membership of half a crown.

In Nailsworth, at the end of the 1920s, there were two policemen, Mr Parsons and Mr Wheeler, who were keen swimmers.

They taught every child in Nailsworth to swim – the learners' section was cordoned off. There were some huts on the site for changing, and they eventually even put up a springboard and diving platform. They had swimming galas and water polo matches there, but I think it was a great shock for some of the other teams, like the Gloucester club, when they arrived. It wasn't quite up to the Barton pool standard!

When we were kids, we swam every day from May to September after school. It was always a competition, as the weather got colder, to see who would be the last to go in. On Sundays, it was only open until 9a.m. so that people could go to church afterwards.

Dorothy Bruton (née Blair), born 1921

The pond used as Nailsworth swimming pool.

Foiled by the Blowers Up

The year of the flood – 1931 – was the last year of the Nailsworth Horse Show. It was always held on August Monday in The Enochs, and it was a big job. Local people took part – they didn't have classy horses to show off. Some came out of the stable, or from off the farm where they'd been working.

They'd have horse jumping and funny races where you'd have to jump off and pick something up. I remember coming to the horse show one day and, when I got to the bottom of the Horsley Road, a lady came up who lived in one of the big houses and said, 'Bertie, I've just seen your cousin win a prize at the show'. My cousin's father was a groom for a millionaire on Minchinhampton Common – Mr Minopria – and I expect he was using one of his horses.

Danter's fair was always at the show with all the belt-driven stuff – roundabouts with lovely music from a steam barrel organ. The steam tractors would work a dynamo for all the fairy lights. Those lights were something for children to see. There were swing boats and games like Roll the Penny and Throw the Ball in the bucket. I'd won at that game three times, when there was a great shout from the fellow manning the stall. Suddenly about six fellows pushed me aside and made sure I couldn't get in again. I think they were called Blowers Up. They were employed by the fair to stop people winning too often. The prizes were only little toys on a piece of elastic.

They always had a carnival on the horse show day. There'd be floats and bicycles all dolled up with ribbons. Brutons used to have one using the horse that pulled their

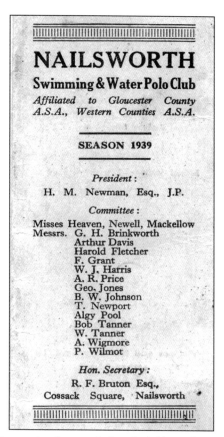

A membership card for the old Nailsworth swimming club.

delivery cart. It was quite something in those days to have a horse to deliver. All the railway goods were delivered by horse. There was a flatbed wagon waiting at the station to take the goods round the area. An old man called Bert Witcombe used to do the deliveries.

Herby Creed, born 1917

Running Away with the Circus

A local girl called Florence Gilliard ran away with the circus. She was quite a bright

115

spark, and there was a lot of talk about it. When her mother died, she had Nailsworth Band to play *Wish Me Luck As You Wave Me Goodbye*, so you can see what sort of a family they were. Florence lived down Park Road, and she had a sort of gypsy look about her.

It was Fossetts Circus, and they always came to the Enochs. They had a big tent, and their elephants would come by rail into Nailsworth station.

Wilfred Hartley, born 1922

Ten To One On The Rovers

I first played for Forest Green at the age of fifteen, for the Reserves, and I finished playing when I was forty. I'd been in the team at the Central School in Stroud and, when I left, I asked Forest Green if I could sign on for them. They had a selection committee, and they would look at your playing while you had a practice, and decide whether to take you on. I wasn't a particularly good player, but I had a long career with the club and always tried to give 100 per cent.

There were no facilities then. The ground was bought by the club in 1932 with an interest-free loan from Owen Davis, the owner of the mill and furniture shop in Nailsworth. I think it was for about £400. All round the ground were hedges and broken-down stone walls, and not much else. We employed a groundsman – an active retired person – who marked the field and put up the goal nets each week. Before the war and afterwards for a bit, it was Fred Porter, who lived in a cottage at Bunting Hill. He was on the committee, too.

Visiting teams changed at the Jovial

Nailsworth Carnival in 1920. The little boy in the picture was so enthusiastic, so the story goes, he blacked himself up with boot polish that wouldn't come off!

Nailsworth football team – before Forest Green Rovers existed – from around the late 1890s. Peter Vick's father, Fred, is in the front row, second from the right.

Foresters, but we changed at home and walked up in our kit. When we played away, we usually changed at a pub. At Amberley, it was the Black Horse. After the match, the publican would fill a bath in the middle of the room with water – and you can imagine what it was like after a muddy game! It was a rush to be the first in to wash. I can't remember them ever changing the water, either.

When I finally finished playing, I ran the reserve side. It was difficult to get people to help, so I used to drive the taxi – one of Charlie Mortimer's – carry the club kit, carry my own kit in case they were short, carry the spare ball and run the line. We were playing up at Chalford once, and I had

changed into my tracksuit to run the line. It absolutely poured down, and I got soaked. When we'd finished, there was this tin bath in the middle of the room – very prehistoric. There was no point in changing, so I just drove the taxi home in my tracksuit!

Ray Stevens, our recently retired funeral director, was captain of the Reserves during their most successful season ever (incidentally, and perhaps significantly, the season following my retirement!), when they won four cups.

Before the war, I was working as an apprentice earning 8s 6d for the first year, and paid 2s 6d every away game to help cover expenses. In those days, you had to provide all the kit yourself. You could wear whatever shorts and socks and boots you liked, but you had to wear the black and white striped shirt, the same as today. Your parents provided the kit, and I expect it was a job as mine brought up seven children, including two sets of twins, and three of the four boys were playing for Forest Green. There was always a rumour that when my twin and I took the 11 plus, one of us failed, and it is obvious to me that I was the one, if the story is right. Well, my parents were as poor as church mice, but, apparently, they paid for one at Central School to keep the twins together.

The club couldn't help players buy any kit because they didn't have any money either. We used to get as many vice-presidents as we could to make a donation – that was your only source of income apart from people paying to watch the game. The vice-presidents would be local businessmen and shopkeepers. The President was expected to write a cheque too!

Before the war, we had a really good 1st XI. Albert Porter was a goalkeeper. He had two sons who were good players – John came from Shortwood to play for us, but later returned to play for Shortwood with his younger brother, Rex. John was a player of County standard and would have won his County 'cap' had he stayed with us. And, as a boy, I used to watch the famous Joe and Gary Brown – two brothers who were full-backs. The Browns were a nice family from Forest Green. 'Scrubby' Cowley played centre half – three of his children later also played football, two for Shortwood and one (also

One of Forest Green Rovers' most successful 1st XIs, pictured in 1936.

Some of the 'local heroes' of Forest Green Rovers: Bob Peachey (top left), Fred Porter (top second from right), President H.J.H. King (centre), Doug Brown (next right), Peter Vick (next right), 'Scrubby' Cowley (bottom, third from left), Ray Stevens (bottom, second from right), Ben Weager (bottom right).

'Scrubby') for Forest Green. Joe Brown's son, Doug, started with me and played for many years. And there was Dudley Vines, a local coal merchant, who played centre forward. He had quite a reputation for being a bit robust. He was a big, raw-boned man, and a rough diamond – all arms and legs. And yet he was an excellent ballroom dancer. Bob Peachey was another well-known player.

Football was more robust then than it is today. A lot of things were allowed, and you were a local character if you made your presence felt. In those days, you could charge a goalkeeper into the net to score. That's one thing about football that has improved nowadays, except that in the old days the fouls were straight-forward – there was nothing sneaky.

There was the odd spar on the pitch between players – and others between supporters. You could always expect a rough game down the Forest – a lot of fouls.

Ben Weager was the 'bag man'. He carried the first-aid kit and attended the injuries. He was a local school attendance officer, so he used to chase you up if you played truant. He came from the Forest of Dean originally, and he played fullback for the club at one time.

Each club provided their own linesmen, so there was no such thing as a neutral one. Nip Beale – his real name was Bert – was our linesman, and he was quite a character. He was well respected as good and fair, which wasn't the case with all of them.

One time when I was running the line at home against a Forest of Dean team, there was a dispute. They alleged they had scored, but I could see the ball hadn't crossed the line. The referee came over and asked me what had happened. To my amazement, he upheld me, and overruled the goal – the opposition were not amused. I was regarded as being fair on the line. You've got to do a job properly.

We'd get big crowds for local derbies. If you played Woodchester, Brimscombe, Chalford or Stonehouse, you'd get five, six or seven hundred people. For other games, there would just be a smattering of people who were interested in the club and players. A lot of the lads used to creep in through the hedge to watch!

The football club was put in hibernation during the war. Brimscombe ran a side that included a lot of people who came home on leave or hadn't joined up. It started again in 1945, though I wasn't demobbed until '47.

In the late '40s, Mr H.J.H. King, the owner of the engineering company at Newmarket, was President. He was a nice man who lived in the big house at Newmarket. He said one day, 'What you really want is a club tie. If you'd like to get one designed, I will pay for it'. That was quite a thing for a club like ours, and that must have been in the early '50s.

I started the first programme we ever had, in the late '40s. I worked at Arthur's Press in Woodchester, and I got it printed there. I went all round Nailsworth and got little 'ads' from shopkeepers. It was quite hard work.

Peter Vick (right) receiving the Stroud League Linesman's Cup during the 1958/9 season, an incredibly successful year when Forest Green Rovers won four other cups besides. The event was well-covered in the local press – note the Stroud News *and* Journal *'proof' stamp on the photograph.*

Nailsworth Band in 1923. Formed in 1919, they wore old Red Cross uniforms purchased for the First World War.

We used to have a Rovers song. It was there when I started playing in the mid-'30s. We would sing it on the coach, in the taxis or at dinners. It probably died out soon after the war ended.

We are the Forest Green Rovers,
Our forwards are hot on the ball.
Our half backs and full backs want beating,
And the goalie they can't beat at all.
Where will they be when the Rovers make
the running?
Where will they be when they've done
their level best?
Where will they be with all their strength
and courage?
Ten to one on the Rovers, and nothing on
the rest!

Peter Vick, born 1921

The Secret of Crystal Palace

I had music in my blood, and I played the cornet. I had no music lessons – I just taught myself. When I was about seven, I joined Horsley Band where Harry Chew was in charge. He wasn't a trained musician but he played the cornet better than anyone else, and that was why he got the job. In 1936, we won our section of the West of England, and we were invited to play at the Crystal Palace – which was a big thing for a little village band. Only the elite played there. We played *Edelweiss* – it was a little waltz, not the piece you hear now.

I remember, I came off the stage after we'd played, and I sat in the audience. A fellow beside me said, 'Who was that bloody band? They were terrible'. I said, 'It was us!' We always joked that Crystal Palace only got burned down because we played so badly!

In the early '30s, we raised money to buy a complete set of instruments from Boosey & Hawkes in London, and we had a concert to christen them in Horsley School. Those instruments ran into thousands of pounds, and it was hard work getting the money. We did various concerts and collections and, of course, we always played down in Nailsworth on Christmas nights. We lost too many players in the war so, when it was over, Horsley and Nailsworth bands amalgamated, and all the instruments went to Nailsworth Band.

Herby Creed, born 1917

Five Shillings' Worth of Riches

There was a great big quarry called Crane Quarry, about 200 yards from Tom Long's Post towards Stroud, on the right hand side. It was walled round, and it served as a refuse tip. It had been used in my time – sometimes Simmonds's men used to go up and extract stone – but they weren't allowed to expand it any further. There was a stone shed, with a corrugated iron roof, at the bottom where they kept their tools. This quarry was just off the fairway of what was then the ninth hole and, if the golfers sliced their ball a little bit, it went down the quarry.

Of course, they had no chance of finding it, so we used to station ourselves there and we would scramble for it. It was quite a steep climb, and whoever got the ball got tuppence. The balls were half a crown new.

On special occasions, the Golf Club would have tournaments, and there wouldn't be enough adult caddies up there. We boys would go up and hope to get a 'job'. I once carried round for Lord Westmorland.

He was a very kind man. He used to refer to me as his Cotswold pony. I had to carry all the clubs – and they were quite heavy – and hand him the one he needed. He wanted me morning and afternoon, and, when we had finished the morning round, he wanted to take me in the clubhouse and give me a dinner. But mother had a hot dinner back home, so I would have been in trouble if I hadn't gone home. I had to be back for Lord Westmorland for two o'clock. He gave me half a crown for the morning, and half a crown for the afternoon – that was riches. I expect I wasted it on sweets or going to the cinema!

Stan Dyer, born 1925

A Ticking Off From Ticker

I used to go to the Picture House quite often. There was a Saturday morning show and, of course, we used to have to sit in the cheap seats – the chicken run – right up against the screen so you had to break your neck looking up. There were a lot of cowboy films with a cowboy called Tom Mix. Kathleen Davis used to watch the film and play the piano accordingly. There'd be a girl on screen who couldn't pay her mortgage, tied to a railway line by a baddy, and Kathleen would be playing dramatic music to go with it.

When we were fourteen or fifteen, we thought we were too grown-up for the chicken run, so we had to move back a few rows and pay more.

Every time anyone got up to walk out to the toilet, their shadow would come across the screen. The film used to break down a lot, and every time it came back on, there would be clapping and cheering.

Right: *An old bill poster for Nailsworth Cinema.*

Below: *A crowd gathers outside the Nailsworth Subscription Rooms – later to become the cinema – for the coronation of George V in 1911.*

Ticker Beach ran the picture house and he used to have to stop us youths shouting or laughing too much. He'd come up and say, 'Now then, you lads, you will be out next time if you do that again'. I can't say we took much notice of him.

Herby Creed, born 1917

Mickey Mouse and Barnacle Bill

When I was sixteen or seventeen, I was an usherette at the cinema, which was where the Boys' Club is. The owner was Mr Beach, but he was always known as Ticker Beach. He lived on the Bath Road, and he was a bald-headed man. He used to make us a cup of tea during our break, and he would always put sugar in my tea – though I didn't take it! You got a bag of crisps too. We had to punch each ticket as people came in, then take part off and put that in a cardboard box. All the tickets were in numbered sequence, and Ticker Beach would go through them all afterwards. He had to check all the numbers for tax reasons.

There were three ticket prices: the chicken run was the first three rows where you got a crick in your neck because the screen was right at you. That cost 3d. The next twelve rows cost 6d. Then the balcony, up the steps, cost 9d.

My first memory of the cinema is seeing a Mickey Mouse film there. The tune stuck in my memory:

> Shall I come down and let you in?
> Shall I come down and let you in?
> Shall I come down and let you in?
> Says the fair young lady.
> It's only me, from over the sea,
> Said Barnacle Bill the Sailor.

I was about four or five when I saw it, and I did laugh. I thought the film was so funny.

Vera Skone (née Clarke), born 1927

Anyone For Tennis?

When I was little, I used to long for the tennis parties at Christowe. My sister, Eva, was cook there, and the children of the staff used to be invited to go along and chase after the tennis balls. We used to love it when the balls went in the strawberry beds. I won't say why!

We loved seeing all the ladies in their frocks. They had a lot of Cotswold stone walls at Christowe, and it was the housemaids' job to scrub those walls so the ladies could sit on them.

We children were given Kunzle cakes afterwards – they were a bit like Mr Kipling – ordered especially from Cheltenham by Mrs Woollcombe-Boyce. We would never have had them in Minchinhampton.

Anne's grandfather, Mr Woollcombe-Boyce, was a lovely man. He was always very particular about the clocks – he had ever so many in his house – and they all had to strike at the right time. As he went to church, through the lych gate, he would pull out his pocket watch from his waistcoat, and check the church clock. He'd always tell my father if the clock was at all out. Mind you, my father would always deny it. Minchinhampton clock was perfect. If it didn't strike with the pips on the wireless, then, as far as he was concerned, it was the pips that were wrong!

My father used to wind the clock by hand twice a week – on Wednesday evenings and Sunday mornings. He had to climb up a ladder to do it, and he hated heights.

No-one else was allowed to touch that clock. If he ever went on holiday, it would be after the clock was wound, and before it was due again. When he was very ill in Cheltenham Hospital, the clock was one of his main concerns. Even the bus drivers used to say that Hampton clock was the only one that was right.

Jessie Kirby, born 1909

Ironing the Billiard Table

The Institute in Minchinhampton was built in 1907, with the main aim of keeping young men off the streets and out of the pubs. It was well used during those early years up to and during the war, and it was only a few pence to join – membership by annual subscription. It was open six nights a week, and there was table tennis upstairs, billiards, darts and draughts downstairs. One of the upstairs rooms was a kind of museum, but I don't remember it being used very much, and it was always kept locked. It housed some very weird stuffed creatures – a small crocodile, a duck-billed platypus, a large round fish that looked like a balloon with spines sticking out all over it, and animals' skulls, and various bits of World War One memorabilia. This room always smelled very musty.

The rooms were heated by old-fashioned cast-iron gas radiators, heated from underneath by a gas burner which we lit manually with matches. There was one big radiator in the billiard room, and smaller ones elsewhere, and I can remember how the walls used to run with condensation on cold, winter nights.

Billiards was the most popular game, and time limits were set by a wall clock, which

A tennis party at Christowe, with host, Mr William Woollcombe-Boyce, in the centre. The minister is Canon Aikin-Sneath.

rang loudly enough to be heard in the house when time was up. For thruppence, you could have half an hour. Sometimes, elderly members coming in demanded – and got – the use of the table whether the young lads had finished their game or not – such was the way of life in those days.

Dad was a good billiards player, and spent many hours patiently teaching the lads how to play. On very rare occasions, Poppy and I were given a lesson, but normally the billiard table was strictly out-of-bounds to us children. I remember dad brushing and ironing the billiard table, which was full size, to keep the cloth (a lovely emerald green colour) in good smooth order, as there were regular billiards matches between the senior members, and these were taken very seriously and played almost in complete silence. The iron was very heavy, measuring about nine inches by six inches of solid cast iron, which dad heated against the burner under the radiator. When it was hot enough, he carefully drew the iron up and down the table in meticulous straight lines, working from outside edges to the centre.

Iris Dyer (née Ellins), born 1930

High Days and Holidays

I remember going to Guides. We used to have the hats with the very wide brim. We were supposed to steam these brims and iron them until they were as stiff as a board. But no-one told me, and I went with a floppy brim and got told off.

Miss Edith Anderson, who lived with her sister at Quarry Wood in Box, was Captain. She taught us a lot of first-aid as she'd been in the VAD in the First World War. We were taught how to make hospital beds with envelope corners. And we did a lot of tracking in Hazel Wood.

We would go to the district camp every year. The first one I went to, when I was about ten, was at North Nibley. We had bell tents and we cooked over fires. There was a duck pond, which we paddled in, which couldn't have been very hygienic!

Another time, we all caught the train

Dorothy Blair's grandfather, William, (top right), with her father, Randolph, next to him, in a Bruton family group.

from Nailsworth with our rucksacks stuffed full, and we went to Warren Beach on the Solent. I can't imagine what it must have been like taking all us Guides and our equipment on the train all that way.

We children always had wonderful Christmas and birthday parties at home, and we'd invite our friends. We didn't have very much garden, but my birthday is the beginning of May, and I seem to think we always had tea in the garden. In those days, it was warm enough to put on your summer dresses at the start of May.

One year, at Christmas, my mother made our dining room into a woodland scene with dimmed lights, and my brothers dressed up as elves and woodcutters, and I was a fairy. She made all these little mushroom cakes. I imagine she worked well into the night. My mother worked incredibly hard when I think about it.

Mr Dickens had a taxi service by the side of Stokescroft. The first double-decker buses in service were always garaged there overnight. Father used to hire Dickens's taxi on a Whit Monday and take us all to Weston. Dad never had a car – never learned to drive – but two of his friends did, Mr Davis and Mr Denley, and they used to come with their families. We'd take buckets, spades, balls, cricket bats, and some of our friends used to come too, and we'd have a day on the beach.

Dorothy Bruton (née Blair), born 1921

One For the Birds

I was a choirboy at Minchinhampton Church, and we used to attend the choir

Dorothy Blair, as a young guide, with that certain hat!

practice under the direction of 'Dicky' Bird, a wonderful organist, but quite unable to keep the boys under control. I arrived late for choir practice one evening, as did Douglas Dallow (still a resident of Minchinhampton) and, as a prank, we swapped jackets. Douglas was taller than me, and much slimmer, and, consequently, my jacket went round him one-and-a-half times, with the sleeve ends between his elbows and wrists. Whereas, his jacket wouldn't fasten anywhere near round my waist, and the sleeves half-covered my hands. 'Dicky' Bird didn't notice, but Dennis Graham did, and got sent home for laughing!

I remember the choir outings to Weston-super-Mare by train where, on arrival, 'Dicky' Bird would leave us to our own devices while he visited local churches. We had to assemble at a given place and time for the return journey.

Alan Hughes, born 1922

A Strange Dream

My father played the melodeon, and every Old Year's Night we'd sit around and sing. The local shops used to sell a bottle of port – port type it would say – and that was our treat for the Christmas and New Year. Dad used to play songs from before the First World War. I remember one:

One night as I slumbered I had a strange dream.
I dreamed of those valleys and dells.
And I listened with joy as I did as a boy
To the sound of the old village bells.
The log was burning brightly
'Twas a night that would banish all sin
And the bells were ringing the old year out
And the new year in.

Herby Creed, born 1917

A group from Nailsworth, enjoying a trip from Sharpness to Ilfracombe in Devon.